Food from
the Seashore

First published in Great Britain
PELHAM BOOKS LTD
44 Bedford Square
London WC1B 3DU
1980

ISBN 0 7207 1183 5 (hardback)
ISBN 0 7207 1235 1 (paperback)

Filmset in Great Britain by Granada Graphics,
and printed and bound by Redwood Burn Ltd,
Trowbridge and Esher

Food from the Seashore

Kendall McDonald

Line drawings by Kevin McDonald

PELHAM BOOKS · LONDON

Contents

	Introduction: Cut Your Costs	7
1	The Hunt Begins	11
2	Lobster on the Rocks	25
3	Potting the Pools	39
4	Edible and Angry Crabs	56
5	Prawning	70
6	Shrimping	82
7	Mussels and Cockles	88
8	Clams Galore	98
9	Limpets, Winkles and Whelks	107
10	Beach Trapping	115
11	Seaweed Snacks	120
	Index	125

Introduction:
Cut Your Costs

Seafood is becoming more and more expensive. Even cockles, winkles and whelks are moving into the luxury price range. Fish and chips are no longer a cheap end to an evening at the cinema. And as for crab and lobster. . .!

Yet seafood is plentiful and easily available to anyone with the know-how to take it for themselves. A little equipment, a little thought and a little effort are all that is required.

Very few people in this country live more than a hundred miles from the sea, and most are much closer. Practically all of us at one time or another during the year visit the seaside. We are then within a few yards of the opportunity to collect enough for several meals. With luck and patience we can collect enough to fill our freezer with the wherewithal for delicious seafood meals throughout the winter.

It takes a lot to make the British seaside holidaymaker alter his habits, but in the past few years patterns have changed dramatically. Picture the family who rent accommodation at the seaside. It may be guest house, small hotel, farm, private house, cottage or caravan. The highlight of that holiday, particularly for those families who were doing their own catering, used to be a meal out — and almost invariably the choice was lobster or crab salad. Well, it must be nice and fresh so close to the sea mustn't it? And it won't be very expensive, will it, with that nice fisherman landing his catch close by?

Well, yes . . . it will be nice and fresh, but

nowadays it will be very, very expensive. In fact it is no exaggeration to say that one lobster meal out may well cost a quarter of the bill for the whole family's accommodation for the week. And if the children eat too – well then your poor holiday-maker may find that he pays the same for one lobster meal as he does for the roof over his family's head for half a week. He doesn't do it again!

Don't blame the cafe or restaurant owner. He has to pay the price the market demands. Don't blame the nice fisherman. He can usually make more money by selling his catch to the Spanish or French boats which now call regularly at our ports to buy up our shellfish. Imagine therefore how much, when you've added in the cost of transport, the French or Spanish gourmet is prepared to pay for shellfish that we used to take so much for granted.

In the following chapters you will read of many 'hidden' forms of seafood – as well as the familiar crab, lobster, prawn, shrimp, cockle, mussel, winkle and whelk – which are yours for the taking. The truth is that people who live by the sea and on the sea have, for generations, been taking and eating delicious shellfish which rarely, if ever, find their way into the recipe books, or indeed any book at all.

Here you will read of the ways of catching gapers, venuses, tapes, razors, otter-shells, carpets, angry crabs, velvets, soft clams, hard clams. More importantly, you will read how to prepare each species for the table, and find the recipes to get the best out of your catch. All this in addition to the ways of making the tides and rock pools work for you. Why you'll even know how to eat seaweed! It's delicious when you know how.

This is not a book about line fishing – there are enough books about that to satisfy all demands –

but it is a book about hand fishing. About the way to collect splendid meals without leaving the shore. I won't say you won't get your feet wet – because you will – but you'll certainly get them wet for a better purpose than paddling.

And that purpose is to cut your cost of living. To eat well from the shore. For nothing.

1 The Hunt Begins

When collecting food from the sea, a great deal of time will be spent on and among rocks. For it is the rocks that provide the hiding places for many of the creatures in which we are interested. But if your holiday spot has no rocky places, don't despair. There's plenty of food available on those apparently bare sandy beaches.

The rocky parts of our shores are, however, likely to be the best collection spots for certain foods. They can also be the most dangerous places for the unwary. At low tide, particularly low spring tides, they can extend for miles out to sea and are a fascinating wonderland for the explorer. But when the tide turns it can come racing in so fast that what on the way out were little waterfalls, splashing into calm deep pools, are in moments raging torrents and great swirling lakes.

Safety First
It is easy to lose your sense of time when working your way out over the rocks, but you must realize that on slippery rocks it is impossible to hurry back when the tide has turned. To stop this sort of mishap, which will result in grazed hands and cut knees at the very least, you must buy and use a local tide table. They cost only a few pence at local newsagents or fishing shops.

With such knowledge you can lift food from that sheltered pool behind the big rock and not have to worry that when you scramble up heavily laden and head back you will find yourself cut off from shore by a great salt river encircling you.

Though of course I don't want to put you off in any way, I would be failing you very badly if I did not point out the dangers of the shore.

Those dangers are easily dealt with and avoided if you take simple precautions at the very start of your hunting expeditions. So let us start by listing several things which you might overlook in the excitement of the chase.

First of all, the hunter among the rocks will usually only be working during the summer months, but winter or summer he or she must have a tide table and know the time of low water and roughly when the tide will start to come in. It's worth asking a local fisherman about this as well, just in case there are any special quirks in the sea's behaviour in your chosen area.

Secondly, you should always carry a small pocket compass.

Ridiculous? You're surely not going that far? Well, no, of course you're not. But have you ever sat on a beach in mid-summer and suddenly found yourself completely blotted out by fog from even the sea wall a few yards behind you? You haven't? Believe me, I have. And I've been in a small boat only feet from the beach and lost all sense of direction. These sudden sea mists can clamp down in seconds in the height of summer. The differing temperatures between sea and land are to blame, but the fog may come out of a cloudless hot blue sky.

I wouldn't like to be out on the rocks when that happens, and neither would you. But it could happen, and as some such mists last for the rest of the day, in a zipped-up pocket of your clothing you should carry a small compass, either water-proof, or safely sealed in a plastic bag.

And while talking about clothing, the choice is

yours. But the choice of footwear is not. You will only choose the best for rock work. The best in this case is not expensive. Any sports store will sell you a pair of basketball boots. These tough canvas boots with the comfortable spongy sole, rubber toecap and ankle protection are not expensive, but they will give you the security you need when your foot slips into the awkward crevice in the rocks. Added to this protection is the fact that they will take seasons of immersion in salt water, provided of course that they are washed and dried after each foray.

Which brings us to another safety point. No one but a fool jumps from one seaweed-covered rock to another. You may get away with it close in to shore, when the seaweed has dried black in the sun to a snap-crackle-pop consistency. Try it on to a rock which has recently been covered by the tide and you'll be lucky not to fracture your skull. Moving from rock to rock is a matter of handholds, footholds and careful movement. It is better to lower yourself into a pool to cross it than try any athletic leaps.

There are some other basic safety precautions to be remembered. Of course, you should be able to swim. Not necessarily like a champion, but enough to swim across a gully that has suddenly filled beyond your depth. Remember too that the barnacles and growths on rocks possess razor-like edges. If you are pushed against them by the sea you will be cut. So take care.

Take extreme care too when standing on exposed rocks. Each year some holidaymakers are swept off rocks and drowned by what the Press loves to call 'killer' or 'rogue' waves. This is simply drawing to the attention of the general public what every fisherman knows – that the sea is unpredictable. The trouble usually comes from far out at sea – usually the Atlantic – when swells surge for hundreds of miles before hitting the coast. These ground seas every now and then throw up a wave that is bigger than the preceding ones. Don't think in terms of great monster waves rolling out of a calm. The so-called 'killer' wave which sweeps holidaymakers off the rocks is often no more than two or three feet higher than the ones before it. Funnelled into rock channels it does, however, reach far higher than other waves – and its force is beyond any non-seaman's imagination. So when any kind of sea is running – particularly at high tide – don't stand out on the rocks.

It is difficult to know what you would be doing there anyway, if you were following the methods of shellfish catching in this book. When such seas roll, the beach gourmet is well away from the shore!

For safety's sake too, you should not encumber yourself with much equipment when rock hunting. You need your hook or net – both of which cost little and can be abandoned in any emergency – and a bag to carry your catch. The old army haversack on the long strap is ideal, but any nylon bag, which can be slung round your neck to keep your hands free, will do.

What to Wear

You're going to get wet anyway, as you will see later on, and will have chosen your clothing accordingly.

British seas can be cold – even in the height of summer – and British rock pools are usually full of the same cold stuff. If you're lucky the sun will have warmed the water in the pools a little. But they'll still be cold.

There is nothing to stop you going on a food hunt wearing your basketball boots, swimming trunks and a T-shirt, but I think you'll get pretty cold, especially if you spot a lobster or big crab and need a lot of patience to winkle him out of his hole.

As I said, it's up to you. You could, of course, put on a pair of old jeans – they'd stop some of the scratches and they would add some warmth. But if you're really going about it seriously, then I'd buy or make some neoprene trousers.

It's amazing how times change and how science comes to help us all. I'm sure when I first started rock hunting years ago I never dreamed of the day when there would be a material available that would not only keep me warm in sea pools but would also act as a cushion against the sharp edges of the rocks. On the other hand, you must realize that the first manufacturers of neoprene never thought of me shivering in my Cornish pools, and how their material could help me.

What we are talking about, of course, is the diver's or water-skier's wet-suit. It may be that for our exploration of the rocks we'll only need the trousers of such a suit, but I must confess I now use a full suit – top and trousers – as I can't stand the sudden rush of cold water over the top of just a pair of trousers!

These wet-suits – please don't call them rubber suits, because they aren't – are made from neoprene, a material which contains a foam-like mass of tiny bubbles. The bubbles act as insulators in the same way that a string vest worn under other clothing traps pockets of air in its mesh. Wet-suits are not designed to keep the water out – in fact they are made to let the water in.

The idea is to have a close-fitting suit whose tight fit allows only a tiny film of water to enter and cover the body. But because of the tight fit no more water can enter once the tiny space between the skin and the neoprene is filled. Your body is a most efficient heat producer and quickly warms this tiny layer of water. Result: you are swimming in your own warm bath.

The first time I ever wore one of these suits I knew all about the theory of why it kept you warm. But the lake in which I was about to test the suit was getting to the crunchy stage around the edges where ice was beginning to form. I doubted very much that I was going to be in for long. No suit could keep you warm in that.

To my amazement I found myself, five minutes later, floating happily around in the water blissfully warm. My hands of course had started off being cold, but as the rest of my body was warm so my hands soon warmed up too. The explanation for this is that when your body becomes cold it 'withdraws' circulation from the extremities in a campaign to keep your vital central parts warm. It isn't as simple as that, as any doctor will tell you, but basically this is what happens. So if your body is warm, the extremities – hands and feet – are less difficult to warm.

There is no need for you to carry out the freezing lake test that I did, you can take my word for it. And you can also take my word for it that the wet-suit is going to be a great comfort to you if you are going to mess about in rock pools or gullies.

If you decide you need a wet-suit, how are you going to get hold of one? There are only two ways – to make it yourself or to buy one ready made. They are quite simple to make and a little further on in this book I will tell you how.

First let us deal with buying a wet-suit. There are many types on sale. The main difference between them is in the thickness of the neoprene material. The thin 3mm thickness is, in my opinion, not quite thick enough for British waters. You need the 4mm or 5mm to guarantee you stay really warm. I use a 5mm and have never felt cold in the seas off Britain. If you plan mid-winter hunting, however, I suggest you go straight to the thickest material, which is 6mm.

Next you will have to decide if you want it lined or unlined. The lined material has a very thin 'skin' of nylon bonded to the inside and makes dressing so simple that the wet-suit is almost as easy to put on as an ordinary pair of trousers and long-sleeved pullover. A lined suit is more expensive than an unlined one. But if you choose the unlined suit you will need to use plenty of French chalk or heavily diluted baby soap solution to get it on. French chalk is perfectly safe, but be careful with the solutions. Remember you may stay in your suit for a long time. One friend who decided that a washing-up liquid was the answer to all his suit problems found that it removed a top layer of skin when he took his suit off. Very irritating!

Other differences in suits depend largely on the cut. The best do not have a seam coming up the side and continuing under the armpit and down the underside of the arm. This is a potential weakness and is avoided by the better suits that make the arm an entire panel let into the side of the suit. Good suits are glued and stitched over the seams. Tape running down the seams is a debatable addition. The tape – even if made of neoprene – is inclined to stretch at a different rate from the material, and so seams that have been taped can be a source of weakness.

You will have to decide, too, whether or not you want a suit with a zip front. If there is no zip the suit top is put on like a pullover over the head and pulled down into place. The suit top without a zip does have the advantage that no water penetrates through the zip fixing. On the other hand, it is certainly easier to dress in a suit that has a front zip. Water entry can be cut to the minimum with a flap that folds underneath the zip before it is shut.

I prefer the suit top without a zip, but Penny, my wife, uses one with a front zipper. And she has never complained of cold water entry through the zip. It is clearly a case of paying your money and taking your choice.

Some suits have short zips at ankles and wrists. I see no point in this and look on these extra zips as just another thing to go wrong. There is nothing so infuriating as a zip that either won't close or else zips without fastening. On the beach there is no way of rectifying the faulty zipper except a lot of patience or a lot of swearing!

Many suits advertised are specially made to your own measurements. One leading suit manufacturer, Oscar Gugen, tells me that he considers this a waste of money – you are usually charged extra for a 'custom-built' suit. This manufacturer produces a series of stock sizes and says that the man, woman, or child whom his suits won't fit is a rare customer indeed.

Notice that suits are made for children too. This is an excellent idea. If your children have wet-suits then an early holiday out of season becomes entirely practicable. My own children when younger splashed about happily in rock pools and on the beach – as well as swimming – when other children without such suits were either confined to shelter or were blue with cold within minutes.

Buying such suits for children is expensive. So are suits for adults. So this is where we should discuss making your own suits at home.

Neoprene, both English and the sometimes

stretchier French material, can be bought in this country. The best thing to do is to write for catalogues. Your local sports shop will give the names of suppliers. Choose the width, thickness and lining (if required) from this. Each material is listed with the amount necessary to make a complete suit. Don't try and cut down on this, or you'll end up with one leg missing!

Various glues are available for sticking the suit together. Yes, these suits are glued together. With modern adhesives it is more likely that the material will tear under terrific strain than that the glued seam will give away. For my suit making I use Evostick 528, but there are stronger glues on the market. Certainly Evostick is fine for all running repairs when needed. The instant glues are not suitable – water is their solvent!

How then do you go about making the suit? You can buy a pattern and simply cut the material to shape with a sharp pair of scissors, or you can buy a ready-cut kit. But I have never had a failure with the following method, despite the fact that it seems rather rough and ready.

Simply roll the neoprene out flat and then get the person for whom the suit is being made to lie down on it, on their back, with as little clothing on as possible. Now take a ballpoint pen and draw widely around their outline. Draw with the pen held straight up and down. Do not lean the point inward under the limbs.

Remember that the joy of home wet-suit making is that you can always glue a piece in if the rough suit is too small – or, as is more likely, you can always trim extra pieces out.

Glue the outer edges of the roughly-shaped suit together. Now try it on. There will be bulges here and there. Pinch these outward and then cut away ruthlessly. To get a proper fit in the small of the back cut out a diamond in the centre of the bulge which is certain to be there and glue the sides together again. Cut another piece of material to attach to the back of the suit. This comes through the legs to fasten at the front like a 'jockstrap'. This holds the jacket down firmly.

When making a woman's suit, take a dart in each underarm seam level with the bustline and one upwards from the waist at either side. This is the same procedure used in making a dress.

With some trimming here and there you will find that you can make a very serviceable suit for much less than it would cost you to buy a similar ready-made outfit. To finish a home-made suit in a professional way, many people use neoprene tape, which comes in rolls of various widths and colours. I have stated before the disadvantages of taping, but you may think these are outweighed by the professional finish that taping undoubtedly gives the home-made suit.

When making suits for children follow the same procedure. The children will grow out of their suits, of course, but you can make suits for youngsters last longer if you glue in panels down all the seams as they grow each year. There is obviously a limit to how many times you can do this. Here tape does come in useful to cover up such extensions, and if you use a different colour for each child you will stop squabbling over whose suit is whose.

Bootees are easily made by cutting a rough outline of the foot and gluing the two sides together, but the hood is more difficult. Follow the method adopted by suit manufacturers here, or you'll end up with a very tight hood that is painful to put on. This applies particularly to women's hoods.

The professional makes his hood in three parts: two side-pieces and one centre-piece which covers the top of the head. This allows room for the width of the head. If the centre panel is made in a different colour – or taped over to give a different look – you will find identification easy.

After all this talk of keeping warm it sounds ridiculous to warn you against sunstroke, but you do lose all track of time when winkling a meal out of those rocks. A floppy hat will not only cut down the glare on your eyes, but will also ensure that Britain's summer sun does not give you a fit of the shivers, which is always a warning that you've had too much sun on the back of your neck. That is, of course, if it is so warm that you have abandoned your wet-suit or shirt.

Incidentally, Polaroid sunglasses are worth wearing as you clamber over rocks. You really can see better through water when such lenses cut out surface glare.

Now all we need is one last piece of equipment and we'll be able to start hunting for seafood. And though this piece of equipment would seem to be vital for the successful pool hunter, it is amazing to realize that generations managed quite well without.

I'm referring to something that will enable us to see underwater – to see where the lobsters, crabs and prawns are hiding. In other words the simple underwater swimming mask.

In times past, the men who probed the holes under the rocks for their quarry would squint through the clear water and learn to allow for the distortion so encountered. And they managed extremely well with this mixture of half-sight and the feelings transmitted to their hand up the shaft of their net or hook.

Some of course used some sort of viewing box, but most did without even this simple aid. I would recommend that you use a mask, which you can buy in most seaside shops, in one of two ways. Either you hold it with your free hand just on the surface and look through it. Or you wear it as it was designed to be worn and immerse your face in the water to see what you are doing. You may find that you want to use the underwater swimmer's snorkel tube as well, so that you can keep looking without being limited by the length of time you can hold your breath.

What you want is a strong mask that covers only the eyes and nose, is fitted with a thick safety glass, and has fine soft rubber edges where it will fit against your face.

And the snorkel you want is a simple U-tube with a comfortable rubber mouthpiece and no curls or gadgets at the end which pokes out of the water. Go to a reputable sports dealer to buy these items. He will not sell you any of the rubbish that is palmed off elsewhere.

Buy the masks for the rest of your family at the same shop. Sad to say, there are still some children's masks around that have such thin glass in them that they are a positive danger. Make sure the glass is thick and that it is safety glass. Some masks on sale use Perspex instead of glass. This is quite all right, but remember that Perspex does tend to scratch. Now we have got to make sure that the mask is suitable for your shape of face. Faces come in all shapes and sizes. However much he hates it the mask manufacturer knows he has to cope with this, so there is a mask for everyone.

There is a simple test for the right mask for you. And you can carry it out in the shop before buying.

Most masks can be made to fit your face by

pulling the strap really tight. But you will find your face marked for hours afterwards if you do. This is not to mention the pain that goes with an overtight mask after only a short time in use.

So the real way of selecting a mask is to test it for comfort and watertightness – without fitting the strap at all. Do it like this: fit the mask you have chosen over your eyes and nose. Press it against your face firmly. Now inhale through your nose. Take your hands away. A mask which is a proper fit will stay there until you stop inhaling through your nose.

If you wear glasses, there are three ways of dealing with your problem. First of all a pair of glasses with very flat metal side pieces will often fit under the mask without breaking the seal. Secondly there is a small gadget which will hold your lenses in place inside the mask with little suction cups. Or thirdly you can go to some expense and have the correct lenses bonded to the inside glass of the face mask.

Viewing Boxes
If you don't like the idea of putting your face into the water, then you should use a viewing box to see under the surface. Basically this is a wooden box with a glass bottom, and it is easily made. But there is a trick in using such a box. Light shining into the box will make it almost impossible to get a clear view of what is below. So you must get your head well down over the box, almost into it, and then twist the box around until you cut out as much light as possible from falling on to the glass through which you are looking.

The box itself can be any wooden box with the bottom taken out and replaced by a sheet of glass. For practical purposes the glass should be plate.

One of the best boxes I ever owned – stolen unfortunately after several years' use – was a stout wooden one with hand-holes cut in two sides and a heavy quarter-inch plateglass bottom. The weight of the plateglass was an advantage because it pulled the box down into the water and was also strong enough to stand up to rough use.

When this box was stolen, I set about trying to find a simple alternative. I finally settled on a two-foot-high plastic water-jug, cut the bottom out and fitted a three-eighths-inch-thick circle of plate-glass into the hole.

Waterproofing this so that it would stand up to water pressure when pushed down into the sea caused some problems. I finally found that four holes drilled through the glass at the local glazier's were the answer. The glass edges were coated with a sealing compound like Bostik 692 and brass bolts and nuts fixed the glass to the plastic edges of the hole in the bottom of the jug. It leaked a little, but nothing like enough to spoil viewing. The narrowing of the neck of the jug and widening of the lip made light-proof viewing easy and comfortable, and the handle made a good grip for holding the whole thing.

Now we have the right equipment we can start our hunting. In the following chapters, I deal with each food species in turn – where to find them, how to catch them, and how to prepare them and cook them for your table.

Good hunting!

2 Lobster on the Rocks

Despite the fact that the Latin name of the British lobster is *Homarus vulgaris*, which literally means common lobster, there is little common about the lobster. It is our most valuable shellfish. Each year British fishermen land about 800 tonnes of lobsters worth over £2,500,000 at ports around the country. Eighty per cent of that catch comes from within twelve miles of the coast, which makes the lobster a shallow-water dweller, and therefore of course very, very interesting to readers of this book.

Know Your Quarry
First of all, scientists, even today, have limited knowledge about the way these shellfish spend their entire lives. They know, of course, that the

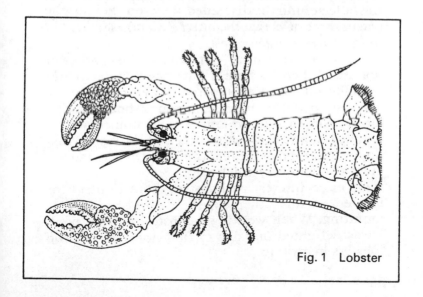

Fig. 1 Lobster

way lobsters grow is by casting off the outer shell once or sometimes twice a year when young. Recently the Ministry of Fisheries' Shellfish Laboratory at Burnham-on-Crouch, Essex, has developed a method of tagging lobsters by which the tag is not lost each time the lobster moults. (If you take a lobster with such a tag do report it. The more scientists learn about lobsters and their movements, the more there will be for all of us.)

The actual act of moulting is fascinating. When the time comes the lobster seeks some suitable hole or shelter. The carapace – that's the body part – splits down the crack line which runs along the back from the beak to the start of the tail section (that's the guide line for the knife when splitting cooked lobsters in two) and the soft creature underneath hauls itself out of the whole shell, legs, tail, eye-sockets and all.

The soft lobster is, of course, particularly vulnerable to all its enemies at this time, particularly the conger eel. The soft lobster shelters in the hole behind the discarded skeleton shell for the two or three days that the outer skin takes to harden in sea water to a new shell.

I am not repeating old wives' tales or even scientists' theories here. I have seen, when diving with the aqualung, an apparently live lobster at the entrance to a hole underneath a small boulder. The lobster turned into an empty shell immediately I touched it, and there at the back of the hole was a floppy imitation of the real thing, not able to move a great deal, but very much alive.

Of more interest perhaps to shore hunters for lobsters is this other experience of shedding or moulting. When working a lobster pot in a pool, I was delighted one day to find not one, but two lobsters in my trap.

However, when the trap was brought to the surface, one of the lobsters looked extraordinary. A pale pinky-white. The other, a navy-blue, seemed very still. What I had was, of course, a lobster that had been trapped in my pot when the call to shed became more than lobster flesh could stand. As a result I had the most marvellous shell of a lobster to glue back together and mount for my cottage wall, and also a piece of duplication that still causes me to wonder. Every single piece of that shell was duplicated in the soft flesh. Left behind were plastic-looking empty eyes, and the tiniest tendrils of antennae ends. And there, complete in every detail, were their duplicates.

I am not suggesting that you should take soft lobsters if you find any in rock pools. Leave them be, especially if they are females, for it is only when the female is soft that the male lobster mates with her. It is then that the female lays her eggs, which are cemented to the swimmerets under her tail. A female carrying eggs is said to be 'berried'. The number of eggs carried by one ten-inch-long female is an astounding 10,000 and the number increases with size. A fourteen-inch female carries some-thing in the region of 40,000 eggs

The eggs will be carried like this for eight to nine months. When they hatch they look like little shrimps, but after five weeks of washing about among other tiny fry, they sink to the seabed and become inch-long lobsters. Now they look like lobsters, but because of their size are not easy to see, and shellfish scientists would love to know more about this stage of the lobster's life. If you do see really small lobsters – or catch one in your prawning net – send a report of your discovery to the Burnham-on-Crouch Shellfish Laboratory. Release the baby first of course.

Lobsters and the Law

While on the subject of size, you must know that the law lays down strict limits of the minimum size of lobster which may be taken from the sea, or rock pool. That minimum size is 80mm carapace length, which means from the rear of either eye-socket to the rear end of the body shell where the tail section starts. You must observe this restriction. If you don't, the fine for landing an undersized lobster can be up to £100. An 80mm carapace length in practice means a lobster of nine inches in total length. It also means that the lobster is about five or six years old.

The law has only recently been changed. From 1877 until March 1976, the minimum size was based upon the total length of the lobster – nine inches long from the tip of the beak (that spiky piece that juts forward ahead of the eyes) to the tip of the tail.

I'm sorry to say that the law was changed because of a practice indulged in by certain fishermen – a slightly undersized lobster was often stretched by careful pulling to make the creature fit the law. This was not just a case of fiddling the law a little. In fact a nine-inch lobster is just about sexually mature. Stretching meant that many small lobsters never had a chance to breed and increase lobster stocks. This sort of stupidity merely meant fewer lobsters for everyone.

The law has recently been changed too regarding the landing of berried lobsters. At one time this was forbidden. But now for an experimental period fishermen can land lobster with their eggs (except in Norfolk and Northumberland, where local by-laws forbid it). This is a case where the law was open to so much abuse that it seemed in most areas of little value. The same sort of unscrupulous fishermen who would stretch a lobster merely took a scrubbing brush to the underside of a berried lobster and all the eggs were gone. Or in some cases not gone but carefully scrubbed into a container and the resulting egg collection sold as a kind of 'caviare'. There is, I am told, very little difference between lobster eggs and the genuine caviare. At least not enough for the uninitiated – which must number most of us – to tell the difference.

Where to Find Lobsters
Anywhere which remains under sea water at all states of the tide. Though you may find an edible crab stranded in a pool that almost dries out, this will not happen with the lobster. A lobster without water is a dead one and, believe me, I have never seen them 'beached'.

You will find lobsters in holes at the very bottom of rock faces, rarely halfway up. You will find them under boulders. You will find them in big tin cans, in long-abandoned petrol or oil drums, broken pipes (some people put down old drainage pipes to trap them), in sunken motor tyres, in fact in and under anything which will give them shelter.

But lobsters are not only taken from hiding places. At certain times of the year – usually at the beginning of autumn – they seem to go walkabout. During my diving life I have suddenly come across them in the middle of a Sahara of sand, far, far away from any rocks, half-walking, half-gliding along. You may well come across them at this time of year between two rock outcrops, crossing the sand floor with a supreme disregard for their own safety. When on this kind of walkabout the claws are folded into a V-shape ahead of the body, which somehow seems to streamline the body – and add menace!

However, do not be fooled by this apparent nonchalance. The slightest aggressive movement on your part will result in those claws being raised immediately into the defence position on either side of the head, and any further aggression from you will result in snapping claws. You should not take this display too seriously – unless you are foolish enough to put hand or fingers within reach. Unlike the small lobsters (up to about six inches in length) which will actually float or dance towards you and try to give you a nip, the big lobster is merely manoeuvring himself into a position for flight.

When he or she decides that discretion is the better part of valour, the flight mechanism will go into action, and very effective it is. The powerful tail strokes up under the belly very quickly, and your lobster disappears rapidly backwards into the distance. As soon as flight starts the claws are lowered to the most streamlined outline and often seem to trail in the water rather than being held rigidly.

Your one chance of catching a lobster in full flight is due to the fact that, despite his ability to look almost behind him from the 'conning tower' position of his eyes, his speed often drives him straight backwards into a nearby rock face. If you are quick, then this instant when he appears stunned is the only moment to capture him.

Picking up a Lobster

There is only one way to pick up a lobster, unless you have no fear for your fingers, and that is to grasp him firmly across the back of the carapace, perhaps including the upper part of the tail in your grip, and hold on. I say hold on because so many beginners, having made the correct grip, are then alarmed at the violence of the lobster's reaction. The tail will arch up backwards, seeming at first to be able to slam down on the back of your hand. Hold firm. . .it can't. Nor can the cutter and crusher claws swing over the back to get at your fingers. But at the moment of grip they do look as though they can. And the lobster will try. The whole body and the tail are extremely prickly, and if you are incautious enough to put your fingers under the tail you will soon find out what a swing of the tail up under the body can do to your hand. Which is why all good lobster hunters wear a stout glove on their grasping hand, and keep their fingers away from the underside of the tail.

What kind of glove? Many pool hunters use a gardening glove, or a stout leather one. The glove should not be too stiff, however, otherwise it will make you fumble that vital first grip across the back. The thin neoprene five-fingered gloves (not mitts) which divers and cold-water sailors use are ideal.

The ones for sailors often have leather strengthening across the palms, which helps. These soft, supple gloves have another bonus. If you are foolish enough to let a lobster or crab claw get a pinch on you, because of the stretchiness of the material you can often slide your finger away inside the glove before any serious damage is done.

How to Spot Your Lobster
First of all, if you venture into the pool looking for some bright red claws sticking up from under a rock, you just aren't going to find one. The live lobster's colouring varies from a bright glowing blue, through navy to black. The sides of the body are often mottled with white speckling on the main colour. It is only when boiled that the lobster turns

that special red that we all know from fishmongers' windows. However, it is difficult to be dogmatic about lobsters' coloration. I saw one in Spain that was a deep dark-brown, and diving friends have told me of lobsters on a rusting wreck that seemed to have absorbed the rust into their body colour. One thing you can be certain of though is the underside of the lobster body and claws. They will always be a yellowy-white.

However, the main give-away sign of the lobster may not be the tips of the claws showing from its hiding place, but the red antennae or feelers, which are folded over the back when travelling, but which when at rest are used as organs of touch.

It is a strange feeling to keep your hand still in front of a lobster in a hole and let him explore your hand with those long red feelers. Curiosity has killed not only many cats, but many more lobsters. He will tend to shuffle forward to make proper use of those antennae, which, though extremely brittle after being boiled by the fishmonger, are very flexible in use and can curl around the contours of your hand. When your lobster moves forward he often exposes enough for a quick grab. I have never been able to find out the exact function of these antennae. I'm sure that they must be for touch only. Whatever their function they are often the real give-away to the presence of a lobster. So you should look for red strands poking out from under rock or weed. They are often such a bright red that they seem to glow in the water.

How Big are Lobsters in the Pools?
I can't answer that; it does of course depend on all sorts of things. But I can tell you that you shouldn't just expect to find small ones. For example, in 1956 a 9½lb giant was taken by hand near Salcombe,

South Devon. Earlier a nine-pounder was claimed from the rocks near Sidmouth, and a 6¼lb specimen from the Western Highlands coast. If you've ever seen a really big lobster, you'll know that taking any of those must have been quite exciting!

But none of these taken from rock pools comes near to the British record for the common lobster. You will hear stories of monsters wherever you go around our coasts. Now adding to the fishermen's stories of the ones that got away are reports from skin-divers of enormous claws poking out of holes in long-lost wrecks. Sifting through all these claims and counterclaims for the biggest of anything is no easy task, but my friend Gerald Wood, editor of the *Guinness Book of Animal Facts and Feats,* is the expert at this sort of research. He has come up with the winner to date – 20½lb! This lobster measured four feet and one-and-a-half inches in total length and was caught in a caisson during the construction of No. 3 jetty at Fowey in Cornwall in June 1931. Its crushing claw weighed 2lb 10oz after the meat had been removed! This giant is the largest so far recorded in British waters. However, with the growth of skin-diving around our coasts it seems likely that even this record will fall in the not too far distant future.

Incidentally, that crushing claw was probably the creature's left claw. The big crusher is usually on that side, with the thinner 'cutter' on the right, but you do sometimes find them with the claws reversed. In rare cases they come with two crushers or two cutters.

When to Catch Your Lobster
Well, in theory you can catch them all year round, especially if extracting them from their holes. But

because the lobster is cold-blooded, its activity is related to the temperature of the surrounding sea. During a mild winter, the lobster may move around a bit and do some feeding, but in a cold winter they hibernate. What we really need for all methods of lobster catching is a cold winter, then when water temperatures rise in the spring, our quarry is very hungry and will come to the entrance of his hole. So I suggest that the best time for pool-hunting is from May to October, with July, August and September as the best months. The time you start wading in the pools really depends on your hardiness, or whether you have a nice warm neoprene suit.

How to Catch Your Lobster
Here we have to deal with several methods, all of which have been highly successful. First let's deal with the one which needs the simplest equipment, and which also must be the oldest method in the world.

For hundreds of years it has been known in this country as fishing by hand. In France they call it *'pêche à pied'* – fishing on foot!

In fact collecting seafood by hand goes back to the earliest days of man. Excavations of prehistoric sites close to the seashore have usually uncovered great mounds of shells such as mussels. So hand fishing was obviously very popular even then.

'Fishing on foot' is only another way of saying fishing without the aid of a boat. The French also have a name for the men who fish the rock pools – *'les bassiers'*. This comes from *'basse mer'* or low water.

In the case of lobsters hand fishing is, of course, no such thing. Well, I suppose you might be lucky enough to grab a lobster or two by hand only from a rock pool, but in fact you do need some equipment.

Gaffing or Clipping Lobsters

Everyone knows what the fisherman's gaff looks like. At its simplest it is a hook on the end of a pole which is used to lift the exhausted fish into the boat after it has been played on rod and line until it is within reach.

To get our lobsters out of their holes – which can run a dozen feet under the rocks – we need something similar. I am not suggesting for one moment that you stride out on the rocks carrying a pole twelve feet long, but you will need some sort of rod with a hook firmly fastened to one end.

Over the years those who hunt lobsters 'by hand' have evolved some extraordinary rod-and-hook devices. They even talk of some hunters being able to turn the lobster round by judicious twists of the hook so that the creature is drawn out backwards ready to be grasped firmly across the back. I do not disbelieve these stories. It just strikes me as an incredible waste of time.

The simplest form of clip or gaff for lobstering can be made from a broom handle. At one end we attach a conger hook. The best method of fixing this is by putting a screw through the eye and then stopping the hook from swivelling by binding it tightly with thin orange Courlene, which you can also buy in hanks from the local fishing tackle shop.

A word of warning. Do not use a brass screw to pin your hook to the shaft. Though it would seem common sense to use something that does not rust in sea water, brass screws do tend to be soft and can snap. A stainless-steel or ordinary steel screw will do just as well. You are going to have to replace the hook at intervals during the season anyway.

The broom-handle gaff is quite efficient. However, after using it for a while you may feel that you would like something more pliable for the twists and turns of the holes.

In this case you should consider a rod of suitable length cut from a hedgerow – hazel when dried is very good – or you can go all modern and buy a length of fibre-glass rod from your fishing tackle shop.

Whatever you choose you are now ready to start. The holes that lobsters really fancy are not the ones facing the open sea. The best holes are often on the shoreward side of the rock, probably because they are the most sheltered. After all it can't be much fun to keep getting bumped by each wave forcing sand into your home.

If you are lucky and can see your lobster, slide the gaff down towards him and underneath him or to one side. He will undoubtedly retreat. Keep the gaff still and it is more than likely that your lobster will reappear. As I said earlier, curiosity has killed more lobsters than cats. The orange Courlene binding will help here. Some pool hunters tie a small piece of white cloth around the shaft above the hook for the same reason. If your lobster does reappear this is your chance. That needle-sharp conger hook if jerked quickly under the lobster (the best place) or under one claw will often stick in so firmly that all you now have to do is to pull your lobster out and into your grasp. If a rock top is handy put him on that before grasping him. But keep the hook driven home or with one flap of his powerful tail your supper will disappear forever.

If your lobster does not reappear, don't despair, You may be able to attract him out in another way. Tap with the gaff on the rock near the entrance to his hole. I have lured many out this way. When he reappears strike again.

However, if there is now no sign of your lobster,

all is still not lost. Hold the gaff gently and slide it into the hole slowly. The lobster is not going to like this thing coming along after him as he retreats. In fact he will not be able to resist counter-attacking. This is the reason for holding the gaff gently. When the lobster's claw (or claws: sometimes they strike with both) grips the gaff or hook you will feel it.

This is where the orange binding helps again. He may well have struck at that, and the hook may be underneath him. Twist quickly and start pulling steadily back.

When your gaff-hook reappears you may only have one of his claws. The lobster can shed his claws at will and grow another one over a period of time. You will sometimes find lobsters with one massive claw and one tiny one in the process of growing. Take the claw off the hook. It's full of good meat. Now try again. Sometimes you will collect both claws before hitting the jackpot.

Warning: if your gaff starts to go mad in your hand, shaking and jerking like a mad thing, try to disentangle and pull out. You've hooked a conger! A small one can be pulled out easily. If it's a big one let him win the day. Keep your hands well away from a conger's mouth. He is unlikely to attack you, but it is best not to tangle with him!

There is another way of using your hook. Lobster holes are often not really a tunnel at all, but a very low overhang. You can tell if this is the case when probing with your hook – the lobster's tail may suddenly appear from under another part of the rock face. You can, if you are very quick, pin him down by his back with your gaff. Or, if you are even quicker, grab him across the back with your other (gloved) hand.

This is the moment when your prawning net would come in extremely handy. With this kind of lobster territory of overhangs and not holes, with the gaff in one hand raking under and the net in the other, you could well drive the lobster out into the net.

When looking down through the water with mask or viewing box all lobsters are magnified by one third, and you may well be disappointed in the size of your catch when brought out into the air. It is for this reason that I have a notch cut in the handle 80mm up from the butt end. With your lobster firmly held down on a rock it is only a moment's work to check that it is bigger than the legal minimum size. Another notch marks the minimum size of crabs – 115mm across the broadest part of the back.

When you find a lobster in a hole and he's safely in your bag, memorize the exact position of the hole. Lobster homes seem to be at a premium, and on your next visit you may well find that another one has taken up the tenancy. A friend of mine who lives in Hampshire goes lobstering at lunchtime when the tides are right. On three consecutive days he found and took lobsters from the same hole!

3 Potting the Pools

This is a way of extending the catching time available to you. Your hunting with the gaff-hook method is, of course, confined to low water. Even that time is shortened by giving yourself the essential safety margin for travelling back without being cut off.

There are drawbacks to putting pots down in rock pools, but we'll come to those in a moment. First, let's look at the kind of lobster pot best suited for our purpose. I think we can discard straight away the traditional pot made in a beehive shape from hazel rods and willow weaving. Fewer and fewer of these are being made, as modern materials are proving stronger and cheaper in terms of labour. Though fine for fishing in deep water, they are less likely to stand up to the bashing they may well get in rock pools, especially if the sea gets up and comes thundering in over the comparatively shallow water. This turbulence is one of the first drawbacks of potting the pools, though we can mitigate it a great deal by careful placing.

Make Your Own Pots
The best kind of trap for our purpose must be the parlour-pot creel. The reason for that is not only the low shape and strong construction of these creels, but also their longer 'holding power' – for it may be some time before we can get back to the spot to recover our gear. I have had to leave these four-foot-long pots in less than six feet of water for as long as a fortnight and they have stood up to it remarkably well. And still held the lobsters!

To make this size buy sixteen feet of 2in. x 1in. pine and cut it into two four-foot and four two-foot lengths. The four-foot-long pieces are the sides and the two-feet-long pieces the ends. Nail two of the shorter pieces across at each end. Now take the other two short bits and nail them across six inches apart near the centre of the base. These act as strengtheners, and one of them will be used for fitting the entrance to the parlour. (Fig. 2.)

The first pot I made in this way I screwed together with brass screws, but this proved to be a waste of time. The brass screws were a bit soft too. Of course nails will rust in sea water, but banging in a few more nails during winter maintenance can hardly be called hard work.

Once the frame is completed, the next job is to find a suitable material for the hoops to hold up the netting. You will need three for each pot. I have used iron strips – coated with rust-resistant paint – curved to a 'U' shape for the hoops.

Wood can be used. So can strong tubing – or stainless steel if you can afford it. But do remember that you are bound to lose a few pots. The thing to aim at is a serviceable pot as strong as you can make it without spending too long or too much on it –

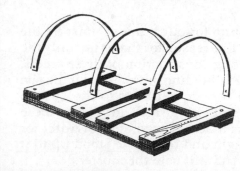

Fig. 2 Making a frame for a lobster pot

otherwise every time you lose one you will suffer a minor disaster. Two or three of the sort of pot I have in mind can be knocked up in a day without much effort.

In each end of whatever kind of hoops you choose to support the netting, you will need to drill one or two holes. Now fix one hoop to each end by nailing or screwing through the holes in the hoops to the outside of the wooden frame where the cross-pieces are fixed. The third hoop is fastened in a similar way to one of the cross-pieces in the centre.

At this stage it does not matter which of the cross-pieces it is. When you have done this you should have a rectangle of wood lying flat on the floor with three hoops standing up from it. The hoops, by the way, should have an archway of more than one foot high at the central point. I do not think the lobster will care very much about the height, having seen the sort of impossible crevices he will occupy on the seabed, but anything less than this tends to be difficult to work – you will want room to manoeuvre when you are lifting your lobsters out.

If you want your pot to last for a long time – several seasons in fact – now is the time to slosh the wood liberally with Cuprinol or some other wood preservative and to coat the hoops with a rust-resistant primer or paint.

Some people say that a lobster dislikes touching metal, but how they know that I have no idea. Certainly I have seen lobsters very happily at home in a rusting oil drum or in the metal debris of a wreck, so I do not think there can be much to such a story. At any rate the metal hoops of my pots have never put any lobster off – and many professional fishermen have abandoned the traditional willow pot for strong metal-wire ones. And they would not do that if it affected their catches!

Back to our pot making. Next step is to get some Courlene fishing net with meshes not bigger than three inches. Fix this to the bottom of the cross-piece to which you have attached the central hoop by hammering in plenty of small staples. When it is firmly nailed down, string it tautly to the top of the hoop and lash it down carefully all the way round the hoop. Use whipping thread and pull the net tight as you 'sew' it through the mesh. Cut any surplus net away. You should now have divided the pot in two and can decide which end of the pot is to be the parlour and which the main entrance.

Repeat the netting the same way with both the other hoops. Now you can see that when we cover the whole pot with netting we shall have two compartments. Both at the moment would allow no entry if we left the netting as it is. Obviously we have got to make entrances for the lobster and also a place where we can put our hand in to take the lobster out. Decide which is to be the main entrance end. Somehow in that netting we have to make an entrance which will allow the lobster to enter, but which will be extremely difficult for him to climb out of again.

As I looked at this stage in my first pot, I felt that a simple entrance spout was not the answer. It would defeat the whole object of the parlour idea. Bridport-Gundry, the famous Dorset fishing net manufacturers, gave me the answer. I wrote to them asking for some suitable netting to make an entrance spout and they sent me some orange polythene twine netting 'ten meshes deep by 2½in. mesh'.

Most important of all, the pieces of net they sent me had the edging loops intact. When you rolled this into a sort of funnel with the loops at the thinner 'spout' end, the stretch and give in the mesh acted like a spring. It was easy to push through, but once through, the edging loops closed together like a gentle spring trap.

The joy of this simple netting device is that it will open up to take the monster lobster, but close again behind him. Any pushing or probing against the net makes it fold back, not open.

To fit this to the netted hoop that you have decided is to be your main entrance is simple. With the whipping twine tie off each mesh of the outer larger end of the funnel to a corresponding mesh in the central area of the netted hoop. Make sure you get a good circular spread. Once the meshes are securely tied all round, simply cut away the net of the hoop inside the whipping. Now you have an entrance funnel leading to the first chamber of the pot. Do the same thing to the central netted hoop. Now you have an entrance into the parlour section of the pot.

The rear netted hoop now needs to be made into a 'door' so that you can reach in and collect your lobsters from the parlour. (If you need to get a lobster from the front section the netting funnel will stretch to admit your hand and arm.) Cut a straight slit in the netting at the rear about eight inches deep. Now tie a piece of cord to the frame of the pot just below the cut. Weave the cord in and out from side to side of the cut meshes, and the whole thing can be laced up in a matter of seconds or undone in the same way. Tie off the lacing cord to the top of the hoop when closing the hole.

Now to the netting. Well, some say any old netting will do – but I don't advise it. Use one of the synthetic ones. They are not only stronger, but practically indestructible – nothing the sea can do will make them rot. In fact it is an unhappy thought that lost fishing nets will go on fishing for ever and ever unless they end up flattened on the seabed, and even then something out for a walk is bound to get caught up in them.

My first pots I covered with the kind of plastic-covered wire that many gardeners use for fencing. Later I found that the plastic did not keep the sea from the wire, and it rusted badly during the second season's use. So then I used Courlene mesh of two inches, and later still tried out some new completely plastic mesh that was once again intended for gardeners' use. That too will never rot.

The method of fixing the mesh is simple. Tack the netting to one of the long sides of the pot with stout staples. Then roll it around the pot and finish off with a row of staples quite near the first. Another row of staples should go in along the opposite four-foot side, and the surplus net at one end is trimmed away from the rear hoop. Now the netting has to be whipped down to each hoop to make the whole thing escape-proof, and the pot is finished. After this I usually spend some minutes admiring my work. There is no doubt about it – a home-made lobster pot is a very satisfying sight. (Fig.3.)

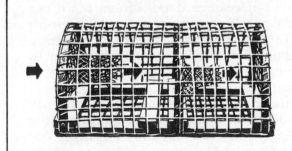

Fig. 3   A finished lobster pot

Fixing the Bait

After you have been admiring your pot for a few minutes it will occur to you that there appears to be no way of fixing the bait in this pot. Do not despair and start ripping all the netting off. I have not forgotten it.

There are many kinds of bait, and we'll go into those a little later on. At the moment though let's look at the methods of fixing the bait in the pot.

The traditional methods used vary considerably. Using the beehive-style pot, the bait is often tied up under the inside edge of the funnel so that the shellfish will have to make a complete entry into the pot and then turn round to get at the bait. Other fishermen tie the bait flat to the bottom of the pot. Some pin the bait down with crossed sticks woven through the mesh; others spit it on a stick which is then forced cross-wise right through the mesh from side to side.

A method often seen is to have a loop of cord attached to the top and bottom of the pot, with a ring of some kind threaded on the loop. The bait is put between the two strands of cord and the ring is forced down, so pinning it in position. Or sometimes you will see a small wooden bait box fixed to the centre of the base of the pot. Holes are drilled in all the sides of the box to allow the bait to ooze droplets of 'scent' into the water.

I experimented with this method for one season, but found it too much of a fiddle. Even the addition of hooks and eyes for easy opening and closing did not seem to me to make the wooden box a very effective proposition. A variation that seemed to have a better chance of success is where the bait box is part of the floor of the pot and can be opened from the underside without having to reach inside the pot at all.

Kinds of Bait

As we have now reached the subject of bait, this is probably the place to discuss the various kinds of lure before going on to show a very simple method of dealing with it.

Basically, there is one rule that seems to apply to shellfish everywhere: fresh bait for crabs; stinking bait for lobsters. This is not to say that you won't get the occasional crab in a pot with high bait, nor a lobster in after fresh bait, but generally speaking the rule works well.

So any fresh fish will do for crabs. Some of course they like better than others, and pot fishermen will often change the kind of fish bait just to tempt some jaded appetites.

An expensive way of buying this sort of bait is to go to any shop with a frozen food cabinet and choose some frozen herrings or plaice. It is, as I say, expensive, but it does have the advantage of being generally available nowadays, even in the remoter places.

It is cheaper to catch your own bait of course. And not so expensive as buying frozen fish is to go to your local fishmonger and get the scraps after he has done his filleting. Shellfish do not care very much which part of the fish you give them, so discarded heads and tails are just as effective.

Bait for lobster pots can be got in exactly the same ways. You have then only the problem of making the fish go off fast. This I do by putting the fish into one of those large screw-topped plastic containers, screwing the lid down tight, and then chucking it into the boot of the car. It is amazing how quickly fish will go off in these circumstances. If you can arrange to leave the container in the sun somewhere for a while so much the better. There will be no smell if you have got a sound container – but please open when well away from sunbathers!

Extraordinarily enough, another bait that lobsters seem to like very much is bacon. At most grocers' shops which handle bacon and ham, you can buy bacon knuckles for just a few pence, and they are ideally suited for bait – firm and strong.

Some professional fishermen have screamed with laughter when I have told them about bacon, but Mr R.C. O'Farrell, whose books about fishing and potting are amusing and instructive, reports that it is highly successful. Certainly it has worked for me too.

Another method of baiting which causes smiles is a tin of cat food. Punch a few holes in it and fix it inside the pot. It works. And it lasts a long time.

Bait Bags

Now for the method of fixing the bait which I consider to be the simplest and least messy of them all. Bait bags. These were pioneered by Mr R.D. Leakey, the inventor of the Leakey Folding Pot, which is ideal for packing in the boot of a car. His bait bags are made of extremely tough nylon mesh. The fish is popped inside and tied into the pot. Each time a shellfish grasps the bait bag, the resulting squeeze releases droplets of bait into the water and attracts more crabs or lobsters. The bag can then be used over and over again.

A more 'wasteful' method which I employ is to buy one of those thin nylon mesh shopping bags and get my wife to stitch it on her sewing machine into eight or so thin, but long, pouches. These last a much shorter time than the professionally made bags, as they are not so strong, but they are quite effective. Greengrocers sell oranges in little mesh bags these days too, and these can be used as they are.

The method of using the bait bags is very simple. Take your piece of fish and pop it into the bag. Now get a long length of any strong string or twine and tie the neck off, leaving two very long ends of string. To bait up, tie one end of the cord to one of the meshes at the top of the pot.

Slip the fish in the bag through the mesh into the pot and tie the other end of the cord to the bottom mesh of the pot. In this way the bait is suspended in the centre of the pot – out of the way of the thousands of small crabs which can cover a piece of bait within seconds of the pot reaching the seabed.

The same thing is done with the knuckle of bacon. Push a sharp knife through between the bones, slip a piece of string through, tie it round the bacon and repeat the method for tying a bait bag inside the pot. If your fish or bacon is too big to go through the mesh, it is the work of only a minute to unlash the entrance at the rear of the pot and tie it top and bottom from the inside.

In addition to my bait bag and piece of bacon, I often add another method of baiting. This means a lot of bait in a pot, but if you are going to leave it down for some time I don't think you can have too much. Anyway fishermen always work on the theory of big baits for big fish. So at this rate one day I am going to catch the most colossal lobster!

The last method of baiting is simply using another product of this plastic age to replace the old wooden bait box technique. Most household stores now carry a wide range of plastic containers. Select a small screw-topped one, punch it full of holes with a skewer, and wire it down to the bottom of the pot.

Then if you want to put extra bait in, it is a simple matter to stuff some fish scraps into the container and screw the lid home.

Positioning Your Pots

So now we have pots and bait. And we have problems. It is not going to be all that easy to get our traps to the potting area if it is across a large area of exposed rocks. It may be that you will be lucky enough to get someone with a boat to bring them in to you by sea. If not, there is nothing for it but to carry them out. In fact they are not heavy, but they will be awkward unless you find one of those gullies that make it simple to wade out floating your pots behind you.

What's that? Floating the pots? How are they going to catch lobsters if they float? Good questions. You see if we had been going to make these pots for boat use, I would have told you how to fix the weights in place. But fixing the weights before setting out over the rocks would really make the whole affair too much of a struggle.

First of all you must realize that though these pots will float well when first put into the sea, the wood will soon become waterlogged, and it will not require so much weight to sink them in position. Even so we have to fix enough weights to keep them down in their brand-new state. To do this we merely make for each pot four bags of fine-mesh net or canvas, take them out with us to the chosen place and fill them there with rocks, stones, shingle – in fact anything heavy which we can find.

Once filled, lash up the open end and attach one bag to each corner of the pot.

Now provided the pots are placed with care, tucked well in on the shoreward side of the rocks – and we don't have the biggest storm of the year before you can get back to them! – your traps should work well. One friend of mine took an extra precaution to make sure that his pots were not moved. He hammered in some of those pitons used by rock climbers and lashed the pots to them. This I think is going a bit far, but it's up to you.

There is another drawback to potting the pools, and this, sad to say, is a part of modern life. Unless you get back to your pots as soon as you can, you may find that someone else has been there before you. I hope it doesn't happen to you, but it has to me. Once I failed to be there when the pots were exposed by a low, low tide, and I'm sorry to say that when I did, the lacing of the parlour on both pots was hanging undone. You can't tell me that the sea could have neatly undone my careful knots. I hope my lobsters nipped him!

Drop-netting for Lobsters

On those days when there's no breeze to ruffle the surface of the sea and all seems calm and still, there's yet another method of fishing for lobsters around the rocks. This one may well appeal to you if you'd like a rest from all that wet work. If so, then it's time to try your hand at drop-netting.

Basically, drop-netting is the art of lowering a circular net with some bait attached to the centre to the seabed near some likely lobster holes.

Out comes the lobster and starts eating the bait. As soon as the creature is in the net, the operator hauls up, the net closes round the lobster, and that's all there is to it.

In fact, of course, it isn't quite as simple as that. First of all you've got to get your drop-net. They can be bought, but they are not difficult to make.

The simplest way is to find an old full-size bicycle wheel. First remove the spokes and you will then be left with a rim with holes in it all the way round. Using the spoke holes, attach a fine-mesh bag of net to the rim. In the bottom centre of the bag you should now fix a heavy weight. Professionally made drop-nets use a circular lump of lead about as big as the saucer of a small coffee cup, with two holes drilled in the centre. This is a good idea because the bait can then be attached by cords through these holes as well as the weight to the bag, but any weight will do. (Fig. 4.)

Make sure that your fine-mesh bag (fine-mesh because it will catch prawns too) is deep enough. It should be at least four feet deep. Lastly fix four short lengths of cord to the rim and lead them upward to a central ring or, better still, double ring swivel.

Now, with your drop-net and enough rope to lower it down from the top of the rocks, plus an air-tight container holding your stale fish bait, you are ready to go. Remember lobsters like really smelly bait – hence the air-tight container! – and crabs prefer fresh bait.

Drop-netting will enable you to fish places you cannot reach by wading, but do remember to take

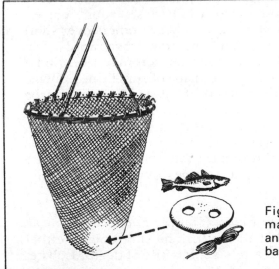

Fig. 4 Home-made drop-net and method of baiting

the greatest care in getting to the point from which you are going to lower the net. You only need to be a few feet above the sea. Remember that the edges of rocks can give way without warning. so this method is not to be used from the tops of cliffs! The sort of place the shore drop-netter should have in mind is the point of a gully in the rocks, the bottom face of which is never entirely exposed at low tide. From this low point you will be able to see down through the water to the seabed.

Lower the net as close as possible to the seaweed edging around the foot of the rocks. Lower it gently so that the weight hits the seabed first and the rim of the net settles around it. From your vantage point you will have no difficulty in seeing the dark shape of a lobster crossing into the net. A crab is more difficult to see. Obviously your chances of seeing movement are much better if a light-coloured netting is used.

When you think your lobster is well and truly in then you should haul away hand over hand at a good speed. If you stop, you'll lose your lobster; remember they are very good swimmers over short distances, even if they do travel backwards. But even if you lose your lobster you may well find a bonus in the net in the shape of some fine prawns. Obviously this method of lobster fishing can be used just as well from an anchored boat.

But whether you use it from boat or from shore, the one thing you must have is a really calm day. If you can't see through the water, then you really are fishing blind. Your chances of a catch then are practically nil.

Preparing Your Lobsters for the Table
Remember that all shellfish must be cooked either alive or within a very short while of death. Lobster

and crab can live quite a long time out of water, and the damp confines of your sack or bag should mean that you get your catch home or to your holiday haunt very much alive.

There is a very long-drawn-out argument still going on about the best method of killing a lobster.

Some experts are quite confident that there is no better or more instantaneous death for this creature than plunging it deep into boiling water. If this revolts you – remember we are talking about total immersion, so do see that the saucepan or vessel of boiling water will take the whole lobster – there are other ways of killing shellfish. The lobster can be killed before cooking by running the point of a sharp knife into the joint between the body and the first section of the tail. This cuts the spinal cord.

Other experts say that the kindest method of cooking and so killing a lobster is to place it in cold water then slowly raise the temperature. They say that during this process the lobster 'goes to sleep' and death is painless. Common sense would say if you adopt this method then you should put some sort of stand between the lobster and the bottom of the pan to stop it resting on the hottest point.

Whichever way you choose, the lobster has to be boiled. The length of time depends on which expert you consult. Some say twenty minutes for the first pound and ten minutes for each subsequent pound. Others say fifteen to twenty minutes dependent on size. Personally I give twenty to twenty-five minutes regardless of size, and I have cooked some monsters by this method without them being in anyway undercooked.

You must boil your lobster in salt water, of course, and though sea water is often recommended it is in fact not quite salt enough. Six ounces of salt to three pints of tap water is about right. The water should be salt enough to make an egg float in it.

Always allow shellfish to cool naturally. Never, never put them into a refrigerator unless you have to.

The next step is to split the lobster in half. It has now gone that lovely picture-cookbook red of course. Press the lobster out as flat as possible on a chopping board – notice how springy that tail is; it's a good test for freshness at the fishmonger's. Now with a sharp-pointed carving knife cut along the centre line of the carapace or body and continue the cut right down the entire length of the tail. Your lobster will now be in two halves. Remove the stomach sac from just behind the mouth, and clear away the black intestinal canal from the tail section. The grey feathery gills are the only other inedible parts.

Personally, I like it just like that, with chunks of fresh French bread, lashings of butter and unlimited white wine. If you want a dip of some kind, the best, in my opinion, is equal parts of Heinz tomato ketchup and salad cream, with a dash of red pepper and a squirt of lemon juice. Your recipe book will, of course, give you many other ways of dealing with lobster. Just be careful that you don't kill the flavour altogether. Some exotic sauces can do just that.

Freezing Lobsters

Contrary to the statements of some experts, lobster meat freezes quite well. The whole lobster does not. I have tried all sorts of experiments with my freezer and lobsters. The important thing to note is that even if you clear all the gills and stomach bag meticulously and then freeze the whole half lobster, you will not only lose a great deal of the flavour, but you will notice that a slight ammonia taste has crept into the meat. This, I am told, is due to the fact that lobsters dispose of their urine through the gills, and however well you clean this part of the creature, minute traces will give this flavour after a period of freezing.

So, if you want to enjoy your lobster later, put only the meat from the tail and claws in the freezer. Even after some considerable time, this will still be delicious.

4 Edible and Angry Crabs

Crabs, like lobsters, are an important resource around most of the British coast. There are, of course, crabs and crabs. There are shore crabs, masked crabs, fiddler crabs, swimming crabs, pea crabs, hermit crabs and many other species, including the spider crab, but we'll come to him later on. The most important, as far as this book and professional fishing are concerned, is the edible crab (*Cancer pagurus*; see Fig. 5).

Edible Crabs
Know Your Quarry

You'll find him, or her, on both rock and mud bottoms from practically nil depth to over 600 feet. Which gives you a fair fishing range to say the least.

Crab fishing is important to both Northumberland and Yorkshire, and has been for centuries. They land some fifteen per cent of the country's catch. Then you have other prolific areas

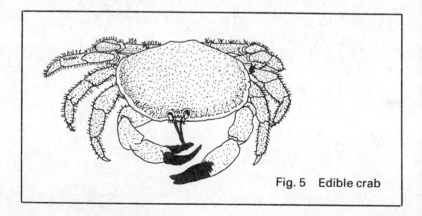

Fig. 5   Edible crab

in Norfolk centred on Sheringham and Cromer. Good-quality crabs come from here and they land about ten per cent of all the crabs taken in England.

But the main fishery in England is concentrated in quite a small area of Devon, which includes Plymouth, Kingswear (Dartmouth) and little ports nearby. It is really extraordinary that this Devon fishery lands fifty per cent of the catch for the whole country.

Perhaps this figure is mainly due to the Devon seamen's persistence. They catch the male or cock crabs close inshore in the spring and then go hunting the female, or hen, crabs some twenty to forty miles offshore in the autumn.

Wales shows up poorly in the quantity chart of landings, but this will change in time. Underwater surveys have shown that good stocks exist off the Welsh coast.

Studies by scientists show that it takes at least four years for a crab to reach the present legal size of 115mm (4½in.) across the back. Crabs increase by an inch every time they moult, but once they reach five inches across the back, moulting is reduced and crabs grow very slowly.

Crabs go for long walks, and the females are the greatest movers. The Shellfish Laboratory at Burnham-on-Crouch analysed the results of tagging crabs and came up with a record two hundred miles for a female which moved from Whitby to Aberdeen. Journeys in excess of a hundred miles seem common, and take from twelve to eighteen months. When you realize that a crab cannot swim, that's a hell of a long seabed walk! On the east coasts crabs seem to walk north. In the Channel crabs tend to move to the west into the flood stream. Crabs from Northumberland head for Scottish waters.

Crabs and the Law

The law regarding the taking of crabs is quite clear, and you must observe it unless you wish to pay heavy fines. You may not take a crab of less than 115mm (4½ inches) across the broadest part of the back.

Where to Find Crabs

In the spring they make their way into shallow waters, and you will often find them in the rock pools left by the falling tide.

You will, however, rarely find them out in the open. Most are either safely tucked away in fissures in the underwater rocks, or hiding under large boulders. Edible crabs will also bury themselves in depressions in sand or mud shores. Only the eyes are usually left showing, but the big depression will usually give away their hiding place. Really big crabs are rare, but plenty within the legal limits can be found.

Picking up a Crab

The edible crab is no joker to play with idly. The claws are immensely strong, and if you are gripped it will not take a monster to break a finger bone. If you are unlucky enough to be pincered, break the claw off with your other hand and smash the attached claw on a rock. Nothing else will release the grip.

Shore crabs will nip and make you jump, but the edible crab is a more serious opponent. Terrible stories are told about people who put their hands into a hole and were trapped by the rising tide as the crab held them fast.

All such stories are rubbish. *But it is true that you should never put your hand into a hole in the rocks.* The edible crab relies to a large extent for his safety on the fact that he is possessed of enormous strength in an upward direction. In other words he can exert enormous pressure upwards from his legs to ensure that he is not tweaked out of a crevice into open water. In the open a crab is at an enormous disadvantage because he cannot swim away – and he knows it.

If your hand is above his shell in a hole you will be trapped against the top of the hole. You will be badly torn getting it out. Get him out into the open, pin him down with your gaff, and he is lost. All you have to do is to grasp him firmly across the back and the claws cannot reach you. Alternatively, if you grab both back legs, the crab cannot bring his claws round to get you either. Even the largest crabs if grasped firmly by the back legs cannot hurt you. But you must grip them firmly and not lose faith halfway through!

How to Catch Your Crab

The thin conger hook-gaff which is used for lobsters may well not be strong enough for crabs. For crabs I always use a length of stainless-steel rod bent round into a short hook. Once the crab is spotted it is really only a matter of hoicking him out from the crack or crevice into which he is settled. Some strength is often needed, which is why your lobster gaff will not last long.

The ideal method of capturing crabs in shore pools is to jerk the crab out into open water and to have your prawn net waiting underneath. The crab cannot swim. In fact he sinks like a brick. If you have the net waiting underneath it is a very simple operation.

Many old wives' tales exist about the method of getting your crab into your bag once you have captured him. I have read that in North Devon they spit in the captured crab's face, which makes him fold up so that he is easily popped into your bag.

Be that as it may, I know that if you put a crab on its back and stroke down the centre of the exposed belly with a knife or gaff, the legs and claws will fold inwards to allow easy stowage. A similar trick can be done with a lobster. If you stroke a lobster's belly with some hard object you can then stand him on his head with the claws forward as triangular support. It doesn't help you to do anything, but I thought you'd like to know!

Potting for Crabs
The method of potting in rock pools is exactly the same as for lobsters. There is one very important difference. The bait must be fresh. Crabs don't like stinking fish as do lobsters. You should also make sure that the entrance holes of your pots are big enough to take a decent crab. Drop-netting works well too. Provided, once again, that the bait is fresh.

How Big are the Crabs in the Pools!
Usually not record-breakers. But big enough to provide a good deal of crab meat for tea. And enough to provide a good deal to put away in your freezer.

But if it's records you want, how about this! In 1895, a crab measuring 11 inches across the back was caught on the Cornish coast. It weighed 14 pounds! And so far as is known that size has never been beaten. In 1972 though, a Yorkshire skin-diver came close with a crab off Brixham, Devon. Though it weighed only 11 pounds its claw span was nearly 37 inches!

If you meet anything like that in the pools, you'll not only set a record, but you'll have nearly enough meat to keep you going throughout one entire winter!

How to Prepare Your Crab for the Table
Once again we are up against the question of how to kill your catch. Crabs can be killed before boiling by piercing between the eyes with a sharp knife or skewer. I do not recommend this method, solely because of my own experience.

I pushed a skewer into a crab between the eyes and then put the crab down, assuming it was dead. To my horror when I turned back to the sink, the crab had the skewer by both claws and was pulling it out!

After that all my crabs went straight into boiling water. You should use the brine method, and the same cooking time as for lobster.

When cold, break off the claws and crack them with some heavy object. Do not use the back of a carving knife – astonishingly enough, you can break the knife in half this way.

Now you have to separate the top shell from the body shell. This is done by simply pulling them apart. If they really won't move, lever with a skewer. Discard the small stomach sac which you will usually find left in the top shell behind the eyes. Throw away the grey gills too. All the rest is edible, and you will need to do a lot of work with a skewer to get all the meat out of the body section, particularly around the leg joints.

Crab meat freezes very well indeed and retains its flavour over a long period of time.

Crabs in good condition – not soft or having recently moulted – are very good value in the way of meat for overall weight. You should get about 10 ounces of meat from a crab weighing 1½ pounds.

Shore Crabs (Fig.6)

Though the edible crab with its dull brick colour and 'piecrust-marked' shell cannot be mistaken for any other, you should not think that only this crab can provide you with food from the shore.

The ordinary shore crab (*Carcinus maenas*) – the one that children catch by dangling a piece of fish on string over the harbour wall – is also edible. The reason that we don't hunt them is because there is little meat inside. But they do make a super crab sauce or soup.

Catching them is simple. Practically every stone you turn over has them underneath. And you can take a tip from the children. A fish head on a piece of string in any suitable pool or stretch of shallow water will provide crabs galore. And they hang on so determinedly that you can easily haul them up into a handy bag or bucket. Shore crabs come in all sizes and colours – from black to green to reddish

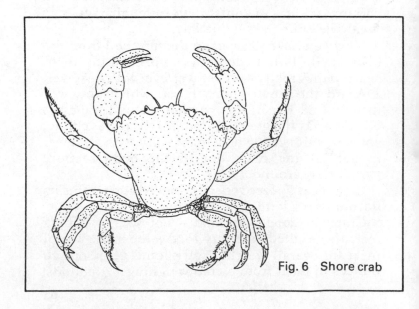

Fig. 6 Shore crab

brown. Don't think because they are small that they can't give you a painful nip. They can and they will.

Now you've got your crabs, for the way to cook them and turn them into sauce and soup I suggest that we turn to one of the best fish cookery books ever written – Jane Grigson's *Fish Cookery*, published by David and Charles.

In her book she suggests turning your shore crabs into Sauce à L'Américaine, which despite its name comes from the land of oil and garlic, Provence. This sauce will be superb with most fish dishes.

Jane Grigson's recipe is as follows: You need:

2lb crabs
1 large onion chopped
1 carrot sliced
1 stalk celery chopped
3 cloves garlic crushed
A bouquet garni including tarragon if possible
¼ pint olive oil
¼ cup cognac
1 cup dry white wine
4 large tomatoes (1½lb approx.) peeled and
    chopped.
Salt, pepper, Cayenne pepper

Wash the crabs. Cook the vegetables in oil until lightly coloured. Add the crabs. When they are red, flame with cognac. Add wine, tomatoes, bouquet garni, and seasoning. Cook for ¾ hour, breaking up the crabs roughly about halfway through. Sieve and reduce the sauce to a good flavour and consistency, adding tomato concentrate or sugar if necessary. Thicken with melted butter and flour.

Angry Crabs (Fig. 7)

The crab which will give you the most trouble in the pools is strangely enough the one the French delight in eating. This is the velvet fiddler or swimming crab – the one the French call *'le crabe enragé'* (the crab in a rage, or the mad crab). The fiddler (*Portunus puber*) is always ready for a fight. His red glowing eyes give you some idea of the state of his temper, and he is possessed of a most powerful nip. The tips of both claws are often a steely colour, and I must say I prefer to avoid a flesh-to-claw encounter. He is covered with a brown pile of closely growing hairs which gives him his 'velvet' name. Where the shell shows through the velvet, it can glow bright blue or purple.

The last two pairs of his legs are flattened into paddles which let him 'swim' or at least dart through the water for his prey.

But his very pugnaciousness – he will sometimes clash his claws over his head like a triumphant boxer (even before the fight), and I have never seen him lose any encounter with a common shore crab –

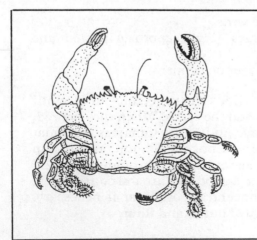

Fig. 7   Fiddler or velvet crab

is his downfall. He will hang on too long to something that takes his fancy, and you can haul him out too.

In the Channel Islands they sell this one under the name of 'lady crab'. In France '*le crabe enragé*' is often part of one of those fantastic '*assiettes de mer*' that you get as a starter to a meal in Brittany – seaweeds, limpets, prawns, crabs, shrimps, carpet shells and all.

The velvet crab is simply boiled for this type of dish and served cold. There is little meat, but by chewing and sucking out the goodness you will appreciate the delicious flavour of these little crabs.

Spider crabs (Fig. 8)
Another crab you will encounter occasionally in the rock pools in summer is the spider crab. Now these really are delicious, and are greatly underestimated in this country. For some reason there is a myth that the spider crab has no meat in him. This is nonsense.

Before we go into the ways of catching spider crabs, let's make sure that we have identified the

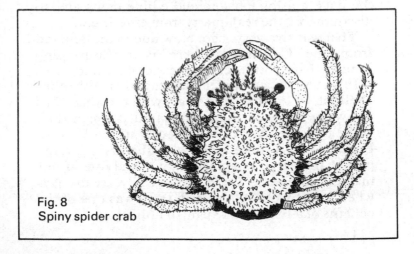

Fig. 8
Spiny spider crab

crab correctly. The one we are talking about is *Maia squinado*, the big spiny spider crab. You will not often find them close inshore, as they love the deeper water, but when you do I must warn you that it is not wise to pick them up by the same method as you would use for the edible crab – across the back or by the back legs. The spider crab is possessed of two good nippers, and unlike the claws of most crabs they can reach round to his back legs. He can also reach right round behind his back.

The best method of catching a big spider crab is to hoick him out into open water and push him into your net or sack. Even so, you will risk getting nipped. His claws are not under such powerful linkage, however, as the edible crab's, and if caught you can simply break off the offending claw.

The spider crab is a master of camouflage, and often sticks weed on to the sharp thorny spikes on his back. You will sometimes find him buried in the sand on the floor of a rock pool.

It is interesting to note that as recently as only five years ago the spider crab was regarded by British fishermen as a great nuisance, getting into the pots laid for lobsters and edible crabs and so discouraging the real quarry from entering.

That was five years ago. Now due to the demand from the Continent, there is a flourishing industry based on catching these crabs alone.

In fact we export spider crabs together with other shellfish to France. And boats which contain just sea-water tanks in their holds find it worth their while to come over to major ports in the West of England to fill those tanks with shellfish. A large part of the cargo is spider crabs – and one of our major customers is Spain! Gone, sadly, are the days when a really cheap shellfish meal was one of the benefits of a French or Spanish holiday.

The reason for this export trade is something that we Britons learned too late – that the spider crab is excellent eating. Some say that the meat is finer than that of the edible crab. I think it is certainly as good, and slightly sweeter.

You will usually find the spider clinging to weed, or upside-down at the entrance to some rock crevice. Upside-down or right way up seems to make no difference to him. He often looks as though he is dead – he can be extremely lethargic – and his colours will suit the surroundings. The hen spider crab, or large female, despite this 'shamming' dead attitude, can, you will find, suddenly burst into life when attacked. The counter-attack can be quite energetic. If you really have trouble calming her down, remember that stroking the stomach with your hook or gaff will produce the same instant curl-up as with the edible crab.

Preparing Your Spider Crab for the Table
Give this crab only fifteen minutes in the boiling brine. Allow to cool. Break the claws and legs off as close to the body as possible. Deal with them in the usual way: crack or disjoint and remove the meat. You will find that compared with the edible crab's strong segments the spider crab's armour is very thin. The body shell comes apart like the edible crab's. Remove stomach bag and gills, and make up your mind about whether you want the brown meat, which in this crab tends to be very runny. It is all very edible, but it does look slightly repulsive.

The best meat in a spider is where the legs enter and are joined to the body. Here you will find great chunks of white meat, and because of the weakness of the shell, the spider is not half so much trouble to clean out as other crabs.

67

Spider crab meat can of course be mixed with that of any edible crab you capture at the same time, but I would advise against this. There is a definitely sweeter flavour to spider meat, and it seems a shame to lose this different taste among other meat. Spider crab meat freezes well. And don't forget that the shells, like those of all other shellfish, are the basis of an excellent soup.

Shellfish Soup
In fact real shellfish addicts will never throw anything away until the last drop of excellence has been extracted. Which is why we now come to the subject of shellfish soups.

The basic ingredient can be the debris from cracking open crabs, the heads and tail armour of prawns and shrimps, the empty shell of lobster, the softer shell discard of a spider crab or two, anything in fact that will give to the soup that shellfish flavour. Obviously if you can spare some of the meat your soup is going to be that much more enjoyable, but a fine soup can be made from shells alone.

For six helpings, you will need, in addition to your shellfish, the following:

2 diced carrots
1 diced onion
Celery sliced
A quarter of a cup of brandy
A cup of dry white wine
4 oz butter
A bouquet garni
2 pts water (or fish stock if you have it)
½ cup of double cream
4 tablespoons rice
Salt, pepper, Cayenne pepper

Cook the vegetables in butter until soft. Add your shellfish bits and pieces. Pour on the brandy. Set alight. Pour in the white wine and reduce. Add the water or fish stock and the bouquet garni, then the rice. Simmer until rice is cooked. Take all out of the pan, remove bouquet if in small bag, add salt, pepper, then liquidize. When you need to thicken, add the cream before serving.

The soup (before adding the cream) can be frozen in your freezer. When needed, heat, then add cream and serve.

5 Prawning

It seems a shame that such a splendid delicacy should have to shelter under not only seaweed but also the Latin name of *Leander serratus*. It is the object of a very determined fishery, as anyone who has had to pay the price of a pint of prawns in winter will know. It seems a great shame that so many fishmongers are now switching over to selling them by weight – they sound so cheap until you realize how few you are getting for your money! The Common Market is, of course, being blamed.

There are several British prawns, but it is the largest, the common British prawn, which is the most important commercially. Generally speaking, you will find them most common on the southern and south-western coasts of Britain.

Know Your Quarry
In life the prawn is almost transparent, and it does not assume that delicious pink until boiled. It is the first two pairs of 'legs' which have tiny pincers and

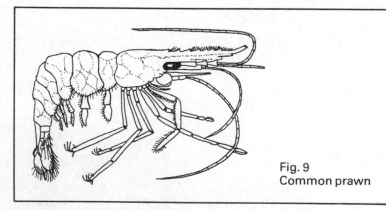

Fig. 9
Common prawn

are used to grasp food and bring it up to the mouth. Other 'legs' are specially made for walking, and under the tail, like that of the lobster, are 'swimmerets' for pushing the prawn forward in a swimming attitude. It is interesting to note that, like the lobster, the tail is the part which develops the most power, driving the prawn backwards at high speed.

Prawns are scavengers, pickers-up of unconsidered trifles, and are ideally adapted to this role. The sense organs are well developed. The antennae search the ground ahead and to the side. The eyes are extraordinarily well developed and mounted on moveable stalks. It is my impression that the prawn can see much, much better than the lobster or crab, but this may be due to the fact that the slightest disturbance of a pool results in immediate flight.

In many ways the prawn behaves like a miniature lobster, but I'm sure the lobster would like to behave like a prawn. Particularly over the question of moulting. Whereas the lobster when young moults twice a year and often yearly thereafter, the prawn takes moulting so much in its stride that in summer it may do so every two weeks. Sometimes if you search a rock pool extremely carefully you will find the cast-off prawn 'skins' everywhere. But whereas the lobster and crabs go through several days of total vulnerability when 'soft', the prawn has speeded the process up so much that it is often soft for only a few hours.

Like the lobster, the female prawn is at her most receptive when soft – the human being has been spared the sight of a floppy female! – and the male, which has moulted earlier, plasters his sperm on the underside of the selected female. Egg-laying follows almost immediately, and the eggs are cemented to the swimmerets. As anyone who has had prawns for tea will know, these eggs are tiny and almost uncountable, but, for the record, there are over two thousand of them on the average female.

The eggs are carried under the abdomen until ready to hatch. Then the small swimming prawn larvae join the other plankton, being washed back and forth until their turn comes to join the adult life cycle. This mating of male and female prawn can happen twice in one season.

Where to Find Prawns
Mainly in the south and south-west, though some good fishing is being exploited in the Western Highlands of Scotland. You will find them in rock pools, often hiding away under the fronds of seaweed around the edges. They like the underside of rock holes at the fringe of the low-tide zone, and often quite a small pool left by the tide will contain as many as a hundred prawns. No cranny is too small for the prawn. Getting them out of such a hiding place may prove to be almost impossible.

How to Spot Your Prawn
It may be that the dark spots which are splattered over the bodies of the common prawn will give them away. But the prawn can change the colour of these spots and change them in size to fit the background. This may seem to make spotting them a very difficult task, but the fact is that, like the lobster, it is often their 'whiskers' which give them away. Your best chance of spotting a prawn's feelers is against a rocky background with no weed to interfere. Once you have seen one, you will always be able to pick out others – even in a heavily weeded area.

How Big are Prawns in the Pools?

Up to four inches, according to some experts. But I can tell you that the largest prawn you are likely to catch in a rock pool or around the fringing rocks of the coastline at low tide will measure about four and a half inches from the tip of the spiky carapace to the end of the tail. If you get one of five inches, you've got a record breaker. Six inches and you're a liar!

It is interesting to note that the spiky portion of the head – the sharp bit that pricks your finger when you are careless about peeling them – is called the 'rostrum', which is the Latin for 'beak'. It also means 'platform', and 'platform' takes its name from the part of the Roman Forum where the beaks or rams of captured enemy galleys were displayed. Which should give you food for thought when you are standing on the platform waiting for a train into which you will be packed like potted prawns!

When to Catch Prawns

It is possible to catch them around the rocks as early as March, when they come in from deeper offshore water where they have spent the winter. However, they usually appear in large numbers later than this, in April and May, and are then plentiful until the autumn, when they leave the shore once again. Some catches are made in November, but the migration usually starts earlier than this.

Old fishermen will tell you that the prawn is particularly sensitive to changes in the weather and will leave the pools for the open sea shortly before a storm and not return until the seas are calm again. It is the sort of old fisherman's tale which is rather difficult to check, as catches are likely to be low as the sea gets up, and during a storm there is no fishing anyway. But as scientists learn more and more about the inhabitants of the sea, a large number of these old tales are being proved true, so I wouldn't just dismiss it out of hand.

How to Catch Prawns
Everyone knows how to do that! You simply get a butterfly net and scrape it under the weed and lift it up. . . Well, no you don't! Not if you really want to catch prawns in quantity that is. Within moments with your butterfly technique, the net will pull out of the handle and you'll be lucky to see even one prawn in the battered remains.

Half the battle lies with the side with the best weapons. It is the same with prawning. You must have a proper net if you are to get the same sort of catches as the expert, who on a good day will get two hundred in an hour and nearly six hundred in a good morning's pool hunting. Not all the prawns caught at these rates are big ones, but it is really not worth keeping the very small ones, as after the prawning comes the peeling and little prawns are the very devil to clean. Mind you, most prawns these days are machine-peeled.

But let's go back to the catching and the correct net. The shape of the rim of the net is a matter of personal choice. It can be circular, square, pear- or even heart-shaped. But whichever shape you choose, make sure that it is big enough and measures more than a foot across at its broadest part.

The most important thing of all is the way the netting is attached. It must hang straight down from the frame. Some prawn nets on sale are very badly made in this respect, perhaps to save on the cost of netting. The netting comes in swiftly from the edges of the rim. All this succeeds in doing is to provide the captured prawns with a trampoline to freedom. With one flip of their tails on this sort of net they are gone, back into the pool.

The mesh of the net should not be bigger than one which will just allow a pencil to slide through. And the bag should be generous enough to allow you to twist the bottom round to keep your prawns inside if, for some reason, you wish to clamber out of the pool before emptying your catch.

The method of attaching the net to the wire frame varies. If you are making your own net, I suggest that you use some method of keeping the netting away from the outer edge, which is going to have to take a lot of scraping on the undersides of rocks. Remember too that the net rim is going to have to take a lot of weight on it – seaweed can be very heavy.

The handle too must be strong, but the average broom handle copes well. It is the fitment of the rim to the handle which is going to have to take a great deal of strain.

To keep the net away from the scraping edge means using a wide band of metal and hanging the net from holes drilled in the inner rim. A local blacksmith – if you can find such a man these days – will be your best bet. Failing that, one of those shops that does decorative wrought-iron work may be able to help you. However, it may well be cheaper in the long run to buy one from a reputable firm like R. and B. Leakey of Belle Hill, Settle, Yorkshire. His prawn nets, for which you supply your own broom handle, sell for a few pounds. The frame is hot-dip galvanized steel, and a black cord plastic fender protects the net from chafing. Mr Leakey also claims that this soft fender stops scraping noises frightening the prawns! His nets come in two sizes, rectangular at 18 x 11 in. and heart-shaped, 13 x 12 in.

Most serious prawn-hunters use the straight handle to the net, but some I know who try to keep as dry as possible bend the net at nearly right-angles to the handle. This enables them to fish under seaweed and into crevices without actually getting into the pool.

Now we are equipped with a stout net, our prawning can start. It really is not just a matter of scooping up seaweed and hoping for the best. There is some skill to catching prawns in decent quantities. Try and spot those give-away prawn feelers in a pool before you start. If you see one at the entrance to a hole or crevice, don't push the net straight at him. If you do, he will disappear with a flick of his tail. Try and slide the net gently underneath him and well past him into the hole. Imagine your net inside the hole. What you have got to do is to make sure that you collect all the other prawns hiding inside – so you must keep the rim of the net in contact with the ceiling as you draw it out. This is easier said than done, and may mean if you make a head-on approach that you have to put the handle of the net right down to the bottom of the pool . . . which is awkward to say the least.

A better approach would have been to slide the side of the net rim into the hole – then you can keep contact with the roof by merely twisting your wrist to right or left. As you pull the net out then you will scrape all the other prawns inside off the ceiling. Once the net is outside, move it swiftly up to the surface and out of the water, then the water rushing through the mesh will tend to pin your prawns deep down in the bag.

When prawning you have to think all the time of ways of cutting off the prawns' escape. This is why when working under a seaweed fringe you should keep the net deep enough in under the weed to remain in contact with the rock behind. If you don't you are just inviting the prawns to escape by getting back against the rock face.

Think of prawns like enemy submarines. When disturbed or threatened, something in the prawn's brain shouts 'Dive, dive, dive!' and down he goes. This is why it is always best to start in the deeper parts of the pool and work upwards. Then at least you can be sure your quarry is going to come down to you. Sometimes disturbing the surface of the water will drive prawns straight into your net.

Though the prawns we buy from the fishmonger are usually trawled up from great depths in northern waters, there is nothing quite so delicious as a bowl of prawns you have caught yourself only a short time before. It is no wonder then that there are many other methods of catching prawns apart from the ordinary handnet.

Clothes-Prop Prawning

You will have read all about drop-netting, which is just as effective for prawns, in the chapter about lobster-hunting, but the strangest method of all is one which I call clothes-prop netting. It used to be practised a great deal in Dorset, but I haven't seen it recently.

It is, I suppose, a form of drop-netting, but the net is much smaller and does not get to the bottom – indeed it floats close to the surface. This is how it is done. A small bag of fine-meshed net is attached to a circle of wire. This rim has three or four short cords which run to a central point. From this point another length of cord of about two feet ends in a round cork float. The bait is attached to the centre of the bottom of the bag. A forked stick, like a clothes-prop, is used to swing the whole contraption out into a rock pool or gully, where it floats around from the cork. (Fig. 10.)

After a short while it is recovered in the same way and the prawns collected. This floating net was also used in harbours where it floated along the walls – a favourite hiding place of prawns – and was particularly effective at night.

As for bait, you could use a stinking fish head or tail, or crushed shore crabs, or, before the onslaught of myxomatosis in Dorset, they favoured ripe rabbit guts. Which may be why they used a forked stick for launching the net instead of their hands!

Potting for Prawns

Potting for prawns is most effective in rock pools and gullies. You can buy pots, and most ingenious some of them are, with as many as five or six little entrances that will admit the prawns but keep out congers and large shore crabs.

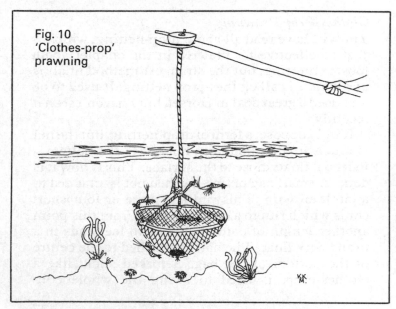

Fig. 10
'Clothes-prop'
prawning

The difficulty with all prawn traps is, of course, keeping the prawns inside for any length of time. The commercially made ones are most effective, but even so you should not leave your traps down for long periods. Some people advise lifting them as often as every hour, which is not possible of course when they are placed in the outlying pools, as the returning tide soon puts a stop to such activity. However, it may well be possible to lower your traps into position from a rock point and recover them frequently. A harbour wall or pier is ideal for this kind of prawning – and prawns love harbours, as the debris from fishing boats keeps them well supplied with food.

You can make your own prawn pots, quite inexpensively, by covering a wooden frame with fine-mesh netting not larger than half an inch square. The entrance holes should be about two inches across and should be cut in all four sides of the netting, so that no matter which way the pot lands on the seabed your quarry can get in. An extra refinement is to stitch into the entrance holes little tubes of stiff plastic net that you can buy at your local general store or gardening supplies shop. This will not only guide the prawns in, but will also help to make it more difficult for them to get out.

Plastic Bucket Pots
Anything will do as a prawn pot. Anything within reason of course. I made some from old plastic household buckets that had started to leak.

A sharp knife cut the bottom out, and then each end was covered with netting. Entrance holes were cut at each end. Two holes made with a skewer in one side gave me a means of attaching the bait inside. Bait in this case was crushed shore crabs (which seems to some extent to put off other crabs from entering), placed inside a piece of nylon stocking and tied in place. A weight (a brick) was tied in position opposite the bait by means of another two skewer holes in the plastic. The lowering rope was run straight through the bottomless bucket and tied off so that the brick was at the bottom side.

This waste-not, want-not type of prawn pot worked well. Oddly enough the white bucket trap seemed more effective than the dark red ones. Fishing was best during summer evenings just around dusk.

Preparing Your Prawns for the Table
Your prawns have got to be boiled as soon as you can. Best take care – the longer you boil them the tougher they get. Prawns can be boiled in sea water, and very nice they are too. But for the very best flavour you need even more salt. In fact you want a brine that is strong enough to float an egg. This can be made by using 6oz of salt (about two cupsful) to four pints (ten cups) of water.

I give prawns just about four minutes in this boiling mixture. The moment they change colour is the best guide. Drain and leave to cool naturally.

When cool, simply peel. But believe it or not, it isn't as simple as that. The experts argue about the correct way to peel a prawn. Method one, which it is claimed produces an incredible rate of peeling per hour (up to 800!), is as follows: Hold the prawn by the head and place the forefinger of the same hand on the prawn's rump. With the other hand uncurl the tail until some plates collapse at the rump. Next squeeze the tip of the tail and give a sharp tug which should pull off the lower segments of plating. With the thumb of the same hand you roll off the plating higher up, at the same time pressing the head with the other hand to make the bared tail drop off.

Or there is this method: Take hold of the creature by the tail and straighten it out. Then press head and tail towards each other in a straight line, and afterwards pull them apart. The entire coat of mail will come away, merely leaving the edible portion to be tweaked from the head.

Get peeling!

Prawns, as you must know from seeing them frozen in fishmongers', freeze well and retain their flavour for some time. They tend to go mushy when thawed if not well dried before freezing.

6 Shrimping

Every guest house and hotel around our coasts has a cupboard somewhere which contains abandoned shrimp nets. The manufacture of these nets would seem to be a profitable business, as old ones are rarely re-used and new ones are bought each season. However, I doubt if two nets in ten ever catch a shrimp, and even fewer catch enough to make a shrimp tea. The reason for this failure is not usually the fault of the nets . . .

Know Your Quarry
The common shrimp (*Crangon vulgaris*) has a flatter body than the prawn, and the sharp spine called the rostrum or beak which sticks out from between the prawn's eyes is missing. The first of the five pairs of legs have pincers – much stronger ones than the prawn's. This is not surprising, because the shrimp is an even bigger scavenger than the prawn. If it's dead or slow and eatable the shrimp will eat it.

Though shrimps are brown when boiled, in life

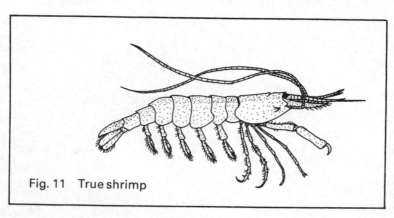

Fig. 11   True shrimp

they are extremely difficult to spot. The fact that shrimps are nearly transparent doesn't help, but it is their ability to change colour to match their background which provides the real camouflage. Shrimps bury themselves in the sand during the day, leaving only two tiny antennae poking up as food detectors.

If you really want to see shrimps in action, your best plan is to throw a rotten fish head into the shallow water covering the sand-mud of a quiet estuary. First to appear will be the shore crabs, of course, and they will attack the bait with great ferocity. But look a little wider afield and through the shallow water you will see the shrimps sneaking in for their share. They walk rather than swim, and it is their movement which will first give them away. At rest they merge in the mud background so well that once you take your eyes away from the spot, you may well not locate them again. Certainly if they snuggle and shrug their way back into the mud you will never spot them.

Like crabs, lobsters and prawns, the shrimp moults. But the shrimp does it fast (getting out of the old plating has been timed at between ten and twenty seconds) and often. In fact moulting takes place throughout the year.

Like the prawn, when winter comes the shrimp moves away from the shore and into deeper water and only returns when the water warms up again in spring. Scientists know quite a lot about this annual movement of shrimps and have discovered that during spring and summer shrimps hatched the previous year make up most of the population. Males and females breed during their second summer and two broods are produced each summer. By mid-July nearly all adult females are carrying eggs.

And it's no wonder that shrimps are common. Females in berry carry from 1,000 to more than 2,500 eggs attached beneath them. The females lie on their sides for the act of copulation.

Where to Find Shrimps

Well, Morecambe or Lytham in Lancashire for a start of course. But renowned as Morecambe shrimps are, you can catch exactly the same kind practically anywhere there is sand, mud flats, or an estuary mixture of mud and sand.

Some get trapped in rock pools and you will often find them among the contents of your prawning net. But generally speaking there is no substitute for the shallow waters at the edge of a low tide. You will not see them of course – just puffs of sand where they have been disturbed and are reburying themselves. You will find shrimps quite a way up estuaries, as they can adapt to the changes of salinity very well.

How Big are Shrimps?

You will find females of up to two and a half inches; males are smaller, reaching a little over two inches. Anything much bigger will be a prawn!

How to Catch Shrimps

The best method is trawling – and that is exactly what the traditional shrimping net is, a beam trawl. But it is a trawl you push instead of towing it behind a boat.

Commercial fishers for shrimps use trawls, of course. They are still pulled by horses in some parts, but motorized tracked vehicles are more likely to be seen now. Shrimps are also netted from boats, and trap nets tied to stakes hammered into the shore are used in other areas.

The shrimp nets bought in most seaside shops are designed for children and are far too small for any enterprising shore hunter, who will probably make his own. I have seen them eight feet wide across the beam, but pushing this giant is extremely hard work and should be left to strong men. The cross-beam should be about four inches wide by half an inch deep. The leading edge should be planed down to make pushing through the sand easier.

A row of stout nails (blunt the points afterwards please) should be hammered through the leading edge. This 'comb' will improve catches because shrimp over which your bar would otherwise pass are driven forward and upward into the net. (Fig. 12.)

The 'comb' has a slight disadvantage in that it will make pushing your net a little more difficult. It is for this reason that I would suggest you try a four-foot-wide net for a start and not go for anything really big at first.

There is really nothing so delightful as walking forward with an incoming tide pushing a well-made and easy-to-handle net before you, confident that when you stop the tail of the net will be full of that moving mound of 'molten glass' that means a really

Fig. 12 Hand shrimp net – the back of the net is tied for ease of transport

good haul of shrimps. And a wonderful teatime spread!

Potting for Shrimps

Exactly the same as for prawns, but there is, of course, no point in setting your pots in rock pools. For shrimp a sheltered creek close to the mouth of an estuary will be your best bet. Bait as for prawn.

Preparing Your Shrimps for the Table

Like all other shellfish, your shrimps should be cooked as soon as possible. Use the same boiling brine as for prawns. It is likely that the shrimp will be done even before the water comes back to the boil, and will float on the surface. Allow to cool naturally, and eat as soon as possible after peeling. Some people do not bother to peel the whole but merely pull off the heads. Peeled is nicer. Shrimps do freeze, but not so well as the larger shellfish.

If you want to keep your shrimps for eating later they can of course be potted. For a pint of peeled shrimps, you should melt 4oz of butter in a saucepan. Put the shrimps in together with a good pinch of powdered mace, a little Cayenne pepper and grated nutmeg. Heat slowly, but do not allow to boil. Pour into small pots. When cold cover with melted butter.

Warning:

However delightful it may be walking barefoot in the shallows when shrimping, please do not do so. Wear plastic sandals or rubber-soled canvas shoes. The reason is that another creature likes to lie buried in the sand as well as the shrimp. This is the lesser weever fish, whose sting can be very painful indeed. The fish lies buried, with only its eyes and the spines on its back above the surface. Where there are shrimp you will often find the weever because it lives largely on shrimps. So take care too when examining the contents of your net.

When the fish is trodden on or alarmed the first dorsal fin is raised and venom from the glands at the base of the spines is injected into the wound. The pain is intense, as my daughter Joanna will tell you. She stood on one in shallow water in Devon. Though the wound will not cause permanent injury unless allowed to become infected, the immediate danger lies in the intensity of the pain causing fainting and falling down. Treat any victim for shock. The best treatment known at present is to hold the affected part in as hot water as can be borne for at least half an hour. Venom from weevers is destroyed by heat. Afterwards the wound should be cleaned, disinfected and covered. In any case see a doctor.

7 Mussels and Cockles

Most people are pretty wary of food in shells, by which I mean mussels, cockles, winkles, whelks and so on. A lot of this wariness is based on common sense. Some of the fear of such shellfish is, however, carried forward in a sort of race memory of days of long ago. Everyone can tell some sort of story of Great-Aunt Agatha either dying or being violently ill from eating mussels, winkles, cockles or the like. What they forget is that the standards of hygiene in the days of Aunt Agatha were generally so appalling that it is a wonder she didn't die from the ham or brawn of which she was so fond – cooked meats containing such seething bacteria that today they wouldn't get out of the factory, let alone on to the stalls from which she was inclined to buy her food.

Shellfish are only as dangerous as the way they are collected, cooked and kept. Modern science and modern household equipment such as the refrigerator and freezer have perfected the way they are kept. The collection and the cooking are up to you. Generally speaking, collecting your own shellfish should ensure that they must be fresher than those you buy in shops. But just to make sure, I consulted Mr Peter Ayres, the Ministry of Agriculture, Fisheries and Food expert on shellfish and public health. He says:

'Mussels should be sterilized in boiling water for three minutes. And I do mean in boiling water. When the mussels are put into the boiling water it will go off the boil, and the three minutes must start from the time the water returns to boiling. I know some culinary experts don't like doing this, saying that it damages the taste and makes the mussels harder, but it is the only way to be safe. [In his opinion the flavour and texture were not lost by this boiling.] You should carry out this sterilization by boiling for all shellfish where you eat the entire animal. Winkles should be given two minutes, cockles three and whelks six minutes.

'Of course, one should not collect from an area that is obviously, visibly, grossly polluted. This is not because the sterilization would not work, but because of the contamination that would be spread about in the actual collecting.

'In certain areas there are local council by-laws about collecting the shellfish due to pollution, and a simple phone call to the Local Environmental Health Officer at the local council will tell you where you would be offending against a by-law by collecting.'

It is an old Aunt Agatha tale that shellfish can only be eaten when there is an 'R' in the month. All this old-time adage ensures is that you get the shellfish in prime condition – not when they are pale specimens exhausted after their annual release of sperm. It also ensured that mussels were not around in a world without refrigerators at the height of summer.

If Aunt Agatha died from eating winkles it was probably due to the fact that they had been pushed around in the warmth on a barrow long before they got into her stomach. And by then they were probably the best typhoid carriers in the world!

The Mussel
Know Your Quarry
The common mussel (*Mytilus edulis*) is really common. You'll find them everywhere around the

coasts of Europe and also on the North Atlantic shores of America. They grow in dense masses and grow quickly. (Fig. 13.)

C.M. Yonge in his splendid identification book to our coasts (*The Sea Shore;* Collins) tells a story of World War Two which illustrates this speedy growth. During the campaign which finally freed Holland from the German occupation in 1944, the sea dykes around the island of Walcheren were breached and the greater part of the island was flooded. A year later when the gaps were closed and the water pumped out, roads, houses and fences were covered with mussels. They even hung in bunches from the branches of drowned trees.

Everyone knows what a mussel looks like. Dark-blue shell, two to three inches long, and attached to rock or other mussels by the byssus, a bundle of short threads formed by sticky fluid running down the long 'foot' which comes out of the shell to plant the fluid on to the selected spot. In sea water the fluid hardens in moments into the tough fibre which you find holding them fast. (Incidentally, this reaction with sea water is the basis of many new glues which are being developed by scientists for underwater use.)

It is all fiendishly clever. The very shape of the mussel is designed to resist the force of the sea. And so is the method of attachment. The threads are

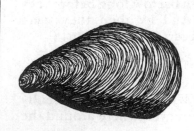

Fig. 13   Common mussel

directed forward so that the pointed end of the mussel swings round to face the pull and push of the tides.

Mussels also tend to attach themselves to themselves, ending up in great masses which save the shore mussel-hunter a lot of time. One good cut with a knife can often slice off a bunch of twenty or thirty mussels at a time.

Here I should say that it is not my experience that the biggest mussel shells contain the largest mussels. The big ones obviously reach a stage in which they are like old soldiers. They do not die, they merely fade away. Some of the largest shells contain a disappointing amount of mussel meat.

Scientists believe that the baby mussel larvae – called spat (like that of the oyster) – settle on the byssus of other mussels because of some sympathetic reaction on contact. This explains the great concentrations of mussels that you find on certain rocks around our coasts.

Mussels do grow larger more quickly in running water – which explains the monsters I have found in places like the Gweek Estuary in Cornwall and the Salcombe and nearby estuaries in Devon. In estuaries the mussels form large colonies attaching themselves to stones in the tidal mud, and it is often possible to pull up a long line or colony by just lifting one small rock. This love of running water causes great problems with power station outlets and inlets. In fact in some such situations the water is chemically treated to prevent mussels settling.

The mussels usually spawn – all together – at full moon spring tides from June to September, and when you realize that one female may eject some twenty million eggs each time you will realize why the keen shore watcher may sometimes see the water go milky!

Incidentally, the horse mussel (*Modiolus mod-iolus*), which is a larger species – growing to five inches in length – is usually more solitary than the common mussel. Its shell is not so sharply pointed, and this rounded 'sharp end' is the way to identify him. Aunt Agatha will tell you that he is not edible. It's rubbish. He is just as tasty.

Mussels feed by filtering the water through themselves and extracting the tiny particles of bacterial food from the sea water. And like everything else in the sea chain of life, someone will benefit from this. The creature which comes out best in this case is the little pea crab (*Pinnotheres pisum*), which lives as a parasite inside the mussel. You'll often find them when you boil up a mussel meal. And the one you'll usually find is the female.

The reason for this is another of those wonderful adaptations of nature. The female pea crab is a pale pinky creature with striking miniature lobster-like claws, but generally a really floppy feeble female. She's a parasite and she lives by scraping meals with her nippers off the mussel's filters.

Pity then the poor male pea crab. When the time comes to breed he has to go dashing around from shell to shell hoping to find a female in an amorous mood. You can tell how tough life is for this Romeo from the fact that his shell is so strong that he can withstand the mussel's shells snapping shut on him just as he finds his Juliet.

The presence of a pea crab in a mussel shell is no reason to reject the meat. In fact the female in America, where she favours the oyster and grows that much bigger, is considered a great delicacy and served on hot buttered toast!

You will sometimes find small pearls in the edible mussel. Don't get excited. They are usually tiny, blue or blackish, and I'm afraid not worth anything at all.

Preparing Your Mussels for the Table
Wash the mussels well. Use a scrubbing brush on those with a lot of growth on them. Discard any that are open: they are dead or diseased. If you can, leave overnight in *clean* sea water, or salted water, to enable the mussels to rid themselves of any mud or grit. This process can be improved if a handful of flour or oatmeal (porridge oats) is added to the water. The mussels will strain this through their filtration system, and out will go many impurities.

Now is the time to cook your mussels. Always – whatever recipe you choose – conform to the sterilizing method of cooking.

With that delicious and simple mussel dish Moules Marinière, for example, the normal method is to clean and beard the mussels (which means to remove the threads of the byssus which are sticking out; a good jerk does it). Then place the mussels in a heavy pan with just a little water over a fierce heat, and remove them as soon as they open.

To include the sterilization method and incidentally to stick closely to the original French recipe, here is all you have to do:

Clean the mussels as before. Put onions, shallots, garlic and parsley (all chopped) together with dry white wine into a big pan. Allow 5lb of mussels to ¾ pint of wine. Let these ingredients simmer for six minutes. Then add the mussels. Bring the liquor *back to the boil for three minutes*. Now transfer the mussels to a collander to drain. Strain the mussel liquor into a saucepan, add salt and black pepper to taste, whisk in some butter, pour over the mussels in a bowl and serve.

While there are a multitude of mussel recipes, it

takes little ingenuity to adapt any of them so slightly that it will not affect the final result to take in the boil-for-three-minutes rule.

All of this care makes it sound as though mussels are a great potential danger. The truth is, of course, that millions of them are eaten each year in this country and all over the world in one form or another without the slightest harm coming to any of those gourmets. On the other hand one case of food poisoning placed at the mussel's door is big news, and it frightens off a number of people who would really enjoy this splendid food. The three-minute rule should enable everyone to eat without fear.

Though the mussel is the most commonly eaten shellfish in Britain, there are many others . . .

The Cockle (Fig. 14)
If you pick up a common cockle (*Cardium edule*) which is over two inches long, you're doing well. The cockle justifies its 'common' title not only by the fact that it is found in the shallows of the Atlantic, North Sea, Channel and Baltic, and in the Mediterranean, but also because of the vast quantities which congregate together. A good cockle bed has been estimated to have over a million cockles to the acre of sand or mud.

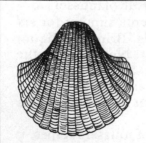

Fig. 14   Common cockle

The cockle reaches marketable size – just over an inch long – in about four years of life. And despite the intensive collection which goes on around our coasts – 300,000 hundredweight a year from England and Wales alone – the cockle continues to thrive.

If, by the way, you find cockles covered with spines, which locals sometimes call red-noses and which are sometimes nearly four inches long, don't despair. Rejoice. You have discovered the Spiny Cockle (*Cardium aculeatum*), and they're just as edible as the common variety.

Know Your Quarry
You can't mistake the cockle – it's a fat shell with over two dozen ribs on it. The shell contains a large foot, by means of which the cockle can bury itself in the sand in seconds. The muscle of the foot is strong enough to flip the cockle out of the water.

I must confess I have never seen this, but I have read of people 'being pelted' by cockles on the move. By accident, of course!

Where to Find Cockles
Anywhere there is fine, muddy sand exposed at low tide. Famous names in cockling stories are Exmouth, Morecambe, Lincoln, Leigh-on-Sea. They do love estuary mud, but do remember that the pollution risk increases in such outlets. Ask locals about cockle beds. Often, as they don't like them themselves, they will tell you where to start scraping.

How to Catch Cockles
Traditionally, all you need, of course, is a garden rake, because cockles do not bury themselves very deeply. But it is not as easy as all that. If you plan to

use a rake – it's hard work, believe me – make sure that the one you get has flat prongs and not thin rounded ones. I say this because often the only clue you will have to raking up a cockle is the clonk of the shell against the prongs, and with the round variety you miss so many.

The cockle shell will not emerge gleaming white. In fact, the detergent-white ones that you find as you walk along the shore will surely be dead ones bleached by sun and polished by tides. The strong shell of the living cockle often looks dull and stained. Don't be put off. If it's shut tight, there will be good meat inside.

A handful of good-sized cockles in the first few minutes of raking gives a very satisfying feeling – rather like a handful of walnuts. In fact some old fisherfolk call them 'sea walnuts'.

There are other ways of catching cockles without raking for them. A small hand-trowel employed in flicking out likely depressions is one. Another, much easier on the back, is to watch the oyster-catchers. These birds are often blamed for eating vast quantities of cockles. Of course they do – they need them to live. But they can also provide you with a good clue to the most prolific cockle and other shell beds. As can the gulls. Watch them. They know where the best cockles are – the closer to the low-tide mark, the bigger cockles you will find – and you should follow their advice.

I gave up raking for cockles some time ago after watching a man walking over the low-tide sands, bending down for just a moment every few paces. The amount of ground he covered was enormous – but then so was his bagful of cockles. For the truth is that if you walk over cockle country and keep your eyes open you will find depression after depression, lying in the centre of which is a nice large cockle. Shallow pools left behind by the tide also have cockles lying on the surface mud or sand. They will only be there during low tide. As the tide comes in they will bury themselves as deep as they can. For then the plaice with his shell-cracking jaws comes sliding in over the sand, and he likes cockles as much as mussels.

How to Prepare Your Cockles for the Table
The trouble with cockles is that they do tend to taste sandy and gritty unless you take care before cooking. It is worth leaving a load of cockles overnight in clean sea water or salted water to clean themselves. It is even more worth while to add that handful of flour or oatmeal to the water as you do with mussels.

Cockles need at least five minutes' boiling in brine, and this should take care of the sterilizing. Remember cockles need three minutes at least for sterilizing from the moment the water returns to the boil.

Cockles can, of course, be used as delicious nibbles between drinks, but are best for flavouring substantial dishes.

Try layers of mashed potatoes interposed with a layer of grilled chopped bacon and chopped cockles in a pie dish and then top off with grated cheese before browning in the oven.

Cockles make an excellent substitute for 'small clams' in the Italian Spaghetti Alle Vongole (Spaghetti with Clam and Tomato Sauce, see page 101). Cook the cockles to sterilizing point. In olive oil, sauté a chopped onion and 3 cloves of garlic. Add 1½lb of skinned ripe tomatoes, chopped. When this has reduced, add the cockles and some chopped parsley. When hot pour over the spaghetti.

8 Clams Galore

Now we move into the world of clams, and open up a whole new gourmet territory – one that has been vastly neglected in this country, and still is! In fact it is only recently that the boom in foreign restaurants has shown us some of the delights of our own beaches that we have been missing. Of course, we have always been proud of our whelks and winkles (we'll come to them later), but we have largely ignored masses of edible shellfish.

The silly thing is that hundreds of thousands of holidaymakers have gone to Brittany or Paris and marvelled at the super shellfish dishes served to them in those wonderful little restaurants which specialize in such delights. But enjoying such dishes is one thing. The fact that those same holidaymakers had walked unknowingly over huge beds of the same clams on their British beaches is another. Only now are things changing. We still go to Italian or French restaurants in this country to enjoy such dishes, but it may surprise you to know that enterprising firms in Billingsgate are supplying those restaurants with the shells from British beaches.

All clams work the same way. They live only inches under the surface of the beach and extract their food from the water by means of the siphons they shove up to the top.

Subject, of course, to pollution, about which I have written earlier, to my knowledge there is no single clam which is poisonous. Some, however, are more tasty than others.

To find clams, you have literally got to rake

around a bit. When you know that the density of these clams on our beaches has been counted in places at over 6,000 to the square yard you will realize that you could strike it very rich indeed. Here then are brief notes on the clams you can find and the sort of territory in which you will find them.

Otters (Fig.15.)

These clams are usually about five inches long. More shell-like than some of the others their Latin name is *Lutraria lutraria*. The shell varies in colour from pink to a muddy yellow. There is a brown outer skin on the living creature, which qualifies it as a soft-shelled clam. It is found all round our coasts, and likes a bit of mud mixed with sand in which it lives. Catch it by digging or raking.

Carpets and Tapes (Fig. 16.)

Really two names for the same creature. The English call them carpet shells. The Latin names for the two most common species are *Tapes decussata* and *Tapes pullastra*. These shells really are very common indeed – in fact they are some of the commonest bivalves in Britain. They like a bit

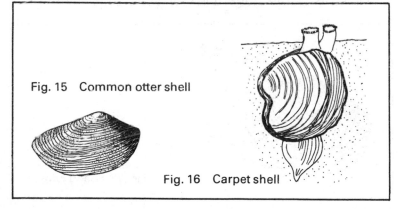

Fig. 15   Common otter shell

Fig. 16   Carpet shell

of muddy gravel, but you can come across huge beds almost anywhere.

They have a stout sandy or brownish shell, with a round front and splayed outer edge. Usual size is just under two inches long. The *decussata* species is only possible to tell apart because it has coarser ridges around it. For this reason it is often called the cross-cut carpet. The other carpet (*pullastra*) often has odd, uneven brown markings. If you really let your imagination run riot you might think that it looked a little like the plumage of a hen chicken, hence its other name of pullet carpet. Both are good eating. Rake away.

Gapers (Fig. 17)
The sand gaper (*Mya arenaria*), though still shell-shaped (as opposed to the long thin razor), is a much bigger fellow and grows sometimes over five inches long. He has a long, long siphon and you'll find him much deeper than the others, sometimes as much as fifteen inches below the surface. This is another one that qualifies as a soft-shelled clam, because of the grey outer skin. You'll see why he's called a sand gaper too when you look at one you've dug out. The shell doesn't close completely because of the huge mass of great long siphons

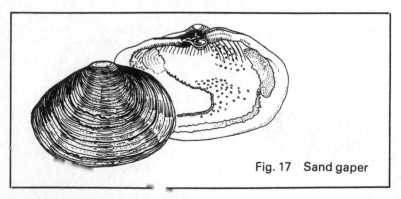

Fig. 17   Sand gaper

which have been pushed up as much as fifteen inches to the surface.

This is the one that the Americans rave about as their soft-shelled clam. Highly prized for food they are there and should be here. To collect – dig. It's hard work but at least you can be sure that he's not going deeper all the time like the razor. Gapers love the sandy mud of estuaries. You'll find them around the low-tide level, and a shallow depression in the mud is the only way to spot them before digging.

Venus Shells

A super one for flavouring a sauce for spaghetti. I was delighted one New Year's Eve in an Italian restaurant in South Croydon to find these lovely little shells still left in the sauce for me to pick out. The proprietor told me that he can now buy them in huge trays from Billingsgate.

Up to two inches across, you'll find them just under the sand near low-water mark. They are whitish, with dots or stripes of brown around them. When you hit a bed you'll find them in enormous quantities. There are quite a lot of divisions inside the Venus species. Best in my opinion for the spaghetti sauce is the striped venus, *Venus gallina* (Fig. 18), but you'll find banded venuses, ovals and warty. All eat well.

For the spaghetti sauce (Spaghetti Alle Vongole) try this for six people:

6lb of clams to one of spaghetti. Brown one large onion and three cloves of garlic in four tablespoons of olive oil. Add a can of Italian tomatoes. Boil down to thick sauce. Meanwhile sterilize your clams then add them to the sauce. Heat for a short while before pouring over the spaghetti.

Razor Clams (Fig. 19)

These also rejoice under the name of razor fish (which they aren't) and razor shells (which they are). They appear to take their name from the old-fashioned Victorian razor, which folds into the handle, but had been known by the name of razor for many years before anyone heard of the Victorians. I don't think you could have shaved with them, but they have a good scraping shape, hence the name.

The pod razor shell (*Ensis siliqua*) at eight inches long is the largest of several in the family – the curved razor and straight razor are the next largest – and all are edible. . . if you can catch them.

Know Your Quarry

The razor clams are good eating, but like many creatures that are good to eat, their defence mechanism is very efficient indeed. The strength of the escape apparatus in the razor lies in the muscular foot and a quick transfer of blood from one part of the body to the other.

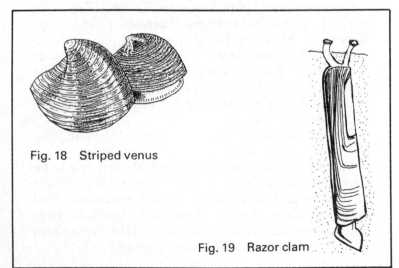

Fig. 18   Striped venus

Fig. 19   Razor clam

When the shell is upright the blood is forced into the body, thus pressing the twin shells outwards against the sides of the creature's hole. Now down goes the foot, blood switches from the body to the foot and the foot swells into a knob. Muscles pull the shell which is now loose in the burrow down after the foot. It's all so quick.

So quick in fact that the hunter, however furiously he digs, is unlikely to keep up. The truth is that you will never see a razor shell until it is dead unless you go about catching them skilfully.

You will find plenty of dead shells in a good sandy-mud environment, but they will be on the surface – a place where you will never find a live razor. The dead shells will undoubtedly have the brownish outer skin peeled away, which will reveal the green-brown shells underneath. Some are yellowish in colour; others have red or violet showing.

Where to Catch Your Razors
You'll find them in any fine sand or mud banks on the fringes of the Channel, Atlantic or North Sea, and in the Mediterranean. The clue to razor shell country comes by walking the ground. Because the razor clams feed by filtering the water, like so many of our sand dwellers, you will often see a jet of water, sometimes as much as a foot high, exhaled at the moment your foot exerts pressure on the sand some distance away.

How to Catch Your Razors
The exhalant squirt from the clams is often your real clue to where they are. When the tide is in they come close to the surface; as soon as it goes out they go deeper. But they do leave behind a shallow depression in the sand in a 'keyhole' shape.

The speed of the razor withdrawing deep into the sand is your problem. Digging with a spade can produce specimens but you are more likely than not to end up with a broken shell, or even a hole two feet deep and the razor shell still ahead of you heading down!

Spearing is one solution. You can make a spear, or have it made, from 6mm mild steel rod. Length should be about two feet to two feet six inches. The point of one end should be flattened so that there is a small barb on each side. These barbs should not be complicated – just projections out of the flattened surface. And you use the spear like this:

Probe for the direction of the hole. It does not always go straight down. You will know immediately – by the freedom of the spear – which way the razor shell has withdrawn. You will know too when you touch the shell. Immediately contact is made, put on pressure and your spear will most likely run between the two shells, because the razor shell is distended in the burrow. Twist and yank back to the surface.

This method is extremely successful. It does usually kill the clam, but it does not matter if you are going to cook the clams more or less immediately. Geoff Bowden, who specializes in this form of hunting, reckons that you should get three dozen razors at low spring tides without much trouble.

Razor clams can also be collected by the 'excess salt' method. This merely means that you add so much salt to the water in the burrow that as the creature draws the salted water through its siphons it is irritated enough to seek the surface. To bring the clam up like this, you need to place a large quantity of salt – a handful – in the depression and hole.

Some people say that this method so irritates the

razor that it even projects part of the shell out of the burrow. Enough in fact for the hunter to grab it. Well, you can. But the brown outer skin is slippery, and you are more likely either to lose the shell and find just a few pieces of brown slime clinging to your fingers, or to get a firm grip and have the shell literally break in half due to the foot pulling down and your hauling up.

Personally, I would never try this snatch method. I have used the salt with some success, but only because after applying the salt to the burrow I then dig deep down and under with the spade. Even after getting the clam out, you should swiftly slip him into a handy bucket – or your razor will be off again sliding under the sand with speed and ease.

Preparing Your Razor Clam for the Table

Clams need to be sterilized like any other shelled food. Give the razor shells at least five minutes from the moment the water comes back to the boil after you have added them to the brine. Razor clams can be eaten as they are, but this I think is a waste. The right place for razor clams is in a recipe for clam chowder.

This American recipe for a Boston Clam Chowder can be varied in many ways, but the basic formula for eight servings is:

1 dozen clams
1 diced carrot
2 cups diced raw potatoes
A third of a cup of diced celery
3 cups of chicken broth (use cubes)
2 tablespoons chopped onion
4 teaspoons butter
2 tablespoons flour
Half a cup of cream
Salt and pepper

105

Put carrots, potatoes and celery into the chicken broth. Cover and boil gently until tender. Cut clams finely with scissors and sauté them and the onion in butter for five minutes. Blend flour evenly into the mixture. Now add broth and vegetables, stirring constantly to keep smooth. Add cream and seasoning. Reheat to near boiling and serve.

9 Limpets, Winkles and Whelks

Limpets

You may think that the common limpet (*Patella vulgata*; see Fig. 20) is a strange thing to think about eating, but that really is because you have known these conical shells sticking to rocks from seaside holidays since you were a child – and no one thought of eating them, did they?!

Once again it seems to have been left to the French to have taken this common rock-dweller seriously in the food stakes. In Brittany in particular you will find the limpet a usual part of the *assiette de mer*.

The truth is that the limpet is very good to eat. It seems to have been a well-kept secret in Britain, though many people who live on our seacoasts have known for ages that limpets are very tasty.

The limpet, which can grow to nearly three inches across, varies in colour through green to bluey-brown, to grey to white. You'll find them on

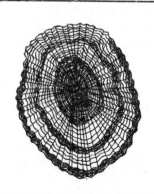

Fig. 20   Common limpet

rocks bordering the Channel, the Atlantic and the North Sea. They live by feeding on the fine seaweed covering of the rocks, and some people say that at low tide, if you listen carefully, you can hear them scraping away. The limpet can survive being left high and dry because of the strength of its foot, which pulls the shell down tight to the rock surface. They also grind themselves into the rock by twisting the shell. You can see the marks left by lost limpets on most sea-line rocks.

Limpets go for 'walks' when fully covered by the tide, but always return to the same spot and fit back into their own niche before the tide rolls back. Television recently showed some fantastic under-water film of these wanderings and the way that each limpet found his or her way back to exactly the same spot.

Any doubts you might have about the strength of the limpet's foot and its ability to cling to rocks are easily put to the test. In fact the limpet has been known to stand a quarter of a hundredweight pull on its shell.

And any doubts too that you might have about the limpet's suitability as food should be put at rest by the fact that the shell heaps left by primitive man in Britain contain not only vast numbers of mussel shells, but an equal number of limpets. Research among early writers has also turned up many references to the 'tons' of limpets eaten around our coasts. Unfortunately they also add that this was especially true of 'the poor'.

Don't be put off. Poor food the limpet is not. But you have got to treat your limpet right. And first you have got to get it off the rock.

How to Catch Your Limpet
Well, you will have no difficulty finding them. The

difficulty is in getting them off the rock surface. The skilled limpet collector takes a tip from the birds. He waits for a relaxed limpet!

Gulls and oyster-catchers are the two main feathered enemies of the limpet, and both look for a limpet which has relaxed its grip, when the shell is raised slightly. The gull gives such a limpet a sideways swipe with its beak. The oyster-catcher slips its bill under the shell edge and flicks it off.

Touch a limpet before trying to get it off and you can forget it. The only way to get it off then is to smash it. The best method is to slip a strong knife under the limpet when it isn't ready. Or to give it a smart sideways blow with the knife handle without warning.

How to Prepare Your Limpets for the Table

One old method suggests boiling them for ten minutes, which certainly takes care of the sterilization. Ten minutes may be excessive; six minutes is more like it. Pull out the two little horn-like tentacles and then eat or mince, slice or chop and fry. Limpet pie is alternate layers of minced limpet (or fried limpet) and mashed potatoes.

Winkles

Now we are into the real snails of the sea. It's odd, isn't it? – people who would throw up their hands in horror at the idea of eating snails have no hesitation in taking up a pin and eating sea snails like the common winkle (*Littorina littorea*; see Fig. 21). We should really call all this family 'periwinkles' to give them their full name. There are four types – common, rough, flat and small.

The one we want is the common variety, which grows up to an inch and a quarter high and is the largest of them all. I don't recommend eating the rough variety because the female retains the eggs until they are hatched, complete with tiny shells, and they say that this gives them a very gritty taste! At any rate all the other varieties are too small to bother about, let alone collect. The rough winkle, true to its name, feels rough to the touch.

In colour the winkle really lets itself go. You'll find grey, green, yellow-brown, grey-yellow, olive, brown, and some with red-brown or dark brown bands.

Where to Find Winkles

Almost anywhere between the tide marks, though they are rare in the Channel Islands and the Scilly Isles. Why this should be is a mystery. I have walked over the rocks of Cornwall, particularly the Lizard, and have seen winkles in such profusion in shallow pools that you could bale them out with a bucket!

No wonder there is a vast trade in our winkles to France, where it seems the demand can never be fully met, even though they have plenty on their

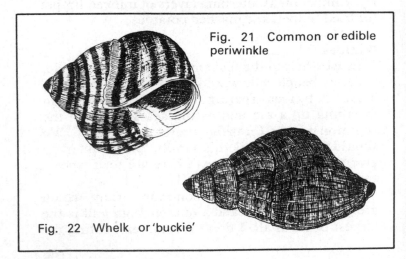

Fig. 21 Common or edible periwinkle

Fig. 22 Whelk or 'buckie'

northern coasts. Kent, Northumberland, Devon and Cornwall are probably the most prolific areas, but the largest winkles come from Scotland and Wales. Tradition says that all the winkles in one pool or on the underside of one rock will point in the same direction. Most I have collected have not heard this! But you will usually find the spire of the shell pointing downwards.

You should start looking for winkles on the rocks from about half-tide level right into the water at low springs. They like muddy estuaries – the Maldon, Essex, fishery is a good example. You'll find winkles on the underside of stones and they have been found attached to tiny pebbles in the middle of sandy wastes.

The winkle 'glues' its shell with a mucus cement to rocks, and so is able to stand the full heat of mid-summer sun, but generally they are more prolific in shady areas.

As anyone who has worked for their meal of winkles with a pin knows, the shell of the winkle is closed with a plate of horn-like material. The plate acts as a sort of drawbridge against intruders, which the animal draws up behind it.

How to Prepare Winkles for the Table
Scrub clean. Boil in brine for anything from two to fifteen minutes, depending on the consistency you prefer. The longer the tougher is the rule. For more tasty morsels boil in court-bouillon (see page 113). Extract with a pin.

Whelks (Fig. 22)
Everyone knows the whelk, the large snail shell that shares pride of place on fish-stalls with the cockle and the winkle. And most beachcombers will know the sponge-like yellow mass of the

111

whelk's egg capsules, which are cast up empty along our shoreline.

But you won't find the living whelk (*Buccinum undatum*) in any of the big shells – up to six inches long – which are often cast up too. All such shells are empty – unless a hermit crab has occupied such a splendid mansion.

The whelk is often called the buckie, particularly in Scotland, but is only fished in a big way around Grimsby and Whitstable. Some whelks on stalls in this country come from Holland.

Where to Find Whelks

Anywhere around our coasts except for the Channel Islands and the Scillies, where they are rare. The really big ones are usually trawled up from deep water, but good-sized whelks will be found at low water in muddy gravel, shingle or soft sand.

How to Catch Whelks

The whelk is carnivorous. It will eat living oysters or other shellfish by forcing the shell open enough to insert its 'mouth' and feed on the contents. It will also eat dead creatures, and one of the most horrifying sights for the squeamish can be produced by placing a piece of dead meat on a muddy surface where whelks are known to be present. Whelks have a keen scent, and soon the mud will heave as the whelks rear up in search of the food.

It is this ability to track food easily that makes the whelk easy to catch. Any kind of small pot placed at very low water with a dead meat bait will catch whelks. All you have to ensure is that the entrance holes to the pot are suitable for the equivalent of a garden snail to crawl into. I have caught over fifty in one go when really potting not for whelks but lobsters. Fortunately the bottom of my pot had a fine mesh, which meant that I didn't lose the whelks when hauling up.

But you really don't need pots for whelks. Simply pile some big stones over a piece of meat, preferably still on the bone, so that it doesn't get washed away, though fish works as well, and on your return you should be able to pick up the whelks clustering on and around the bait. This is another case where a punctured tin of catmeat or dogfood would do the job just as well.

How to Prepare Whelks for the Table
Whelks are eaten boiled. Follow the sterilization rule here and give them at least six minutes from the moment the brine returns to the boil. You can then eat them with vinegar according to your taste. But in my opinion whelks are very tough, and I would give them at least twenty minutes' boiling before eating them.

A much tastier method is to adapt the whelk to the classic French snail recipe (Escargots à la Bourguignonne). Here's how: boil the snails in brine for twenty minutes. While this is going on prepare a court-bouillon with 1½ pts water, 1 onion, 1 sliced carrot, bouquet garni, and one clove of garlic. Now swap the snails over to the court-bouillon and cook for a further fifteen minutes. Let cool. Now take ½lb of butter, some chopped parsley, and two more finely chopped cloves of garlic. Work all together and then add plenty of salt and pepper. Winkle out the whelks. Wash the shells. Place a bit of your butter mixture at the bottom of each shell, replace the whelk, and fill with more butter mixture. Now arrange the whelks and their butter-filled shells in baking dishes and place in a hot oven until they are bubbling away. Serve hot with French bread and lashings of wine.

The method for another tasty dish is to remove the whelks from the shells after twenty minutes' boiling and mince them. Braise some onions and then add the minced whelks. Cook slowly for another fifteen minutes and then serve with rice.

Or how about whelk pie? Grill some bacon and cut into small pieces. Boil whelks for twenty minutes and remove from shells. Chop small. Now put a layer of mashed potatoes in a pie-dish, then a layer of whelk mixed with bacon bits, then potatoes again, and so on. When dish is full, sprinkle with grated cheese and brown in oven.

Any cookbook and a certain amount of imagination will enable the beach hunting gourmet to make superb shellfish dishes. After all, having caught the food yourself, you can afford to experiment!

10 Beach Trapping

As I said at the beginning of this book, it is not concerned with line fishing. But there are ways of catching fish for your table which will probably make the average rod-and-line fisherman speechless with horror. What follows is not intended to be an insult to the skills of the beach fisherman, but merely a guide to other practical methods of taking fish.

The two most successful of these methods are pool baiting in rocky areas and long-lining on sandy beaches.

Pool Baiting

What we are doing here is setting out to catch the congers, which are hiding in the deep holes and come out at night to feed, and other fish such as bass, which move in over the rocks as the tide comes in to snap up small crabs and other delicacies.

The difficulty here is to keep any bait we put down away from the reach of those same small crabs. A piece of bait on a hook with a strong-breaking-strength line attached to it lying on the floor of a pool will often prove useless, because by the time the fish gets there the crabs will have removed every trace of bait.

It is easy enough to fix your line to the rocks – several turns round a handy projection will do – but not so easy to keep the crabs away. However, the following method has worked quite well for me.

Bait your hook. If it's conger you're after, any

fresh fish bait will do. Use a conger hook and at least 20lb breaking-strain line attached to it. To the hook-eye attach another two-foot-long piece of line, and to the other end of this piece attach some form of float. I say 'some form of float' because it is not worth spending money on this float, as you may well lose it. Anything that floats will do – a piece of cork, or an old plastic bottle (well stoppered), for example. Several feet below the bait – depending, of course, on the depth and size of your pool – attach a weight. Now when you put your hook and bait into the water it should float well clear of the bottom and yet be held in position by the weight. Put out several of these baited hooks (smaller ones for bass – size 4), mark the position of each carefully for your return, and leave overnight. With luck, and every fisher-man needs that as well as know-how, you'll be able to pick up a nice conger or bass in the morning. Be careful how you handle a conger. They can go on biting after any other fish would be dead. To make sure, kill your conger by hitting it as hard as you can with a stout stick on the vent.

How to Prepare Your Conger for the Table
First of all don't let anyone tell you that it's easy to skin a conger. Just cut around the neck, they say, give a quick jerk and the whole skin comes away like a glove. Well, it doesn't. Not in my experience at least – but perhaps I wasn't doing it right. I suggest that you cut your conger up into pieces of the right size for the cooking you intend and skin those pieces separately.

Remember whichever recipe you use that the conger is a strongly-flavoured fish and will tend to dominate if you mix other fish with it. You should also remember that conger gives off a powerful smell when being cooked, so shut the kitchen door.

None of this means that it isn't good eating; it is, but use the thick end. The tail is very bony.

Conger can be simply boiled or baked and served with any sauce that takes your fancy. It makes a good fish soup. And in the Canary Islands they cook it with onions, peas, carrots, and a liberal dowsing of sherry.

Beach Long-Lining

This method is unlikely to catch you a conger. It may catch bass as they move in over the sand as the tide covers it. But is more likely to produce a tasty plaice or two. The plaice do the same thing as the bass. As the tide comes in so they like to move in with it to see what uncovered trifles they can snap up.

Long-lining is simply a method of laying a number of baited hooks over a length of beach. It is best to lay this in the evening just before the tide turns. Do not lay it during the day where children paddling might tread on it.

The work of making up such a line is best done at home or in your hotel bedroom (don't get the hooks caught in the sheets!). Remember not to make the line too long because there will be tangles, if not in laying it, then certainly in the raising.

Knot short traces or snoods to the main line every three feet. Keep the traces short, and make sure that they cannot slip down the line. If they do, a good-sized fish will create havoc when trying to escape. In the real long-lining for cod off Newfoundland the lines are hundreds of feet long and have hundreds of hooks, but I suggest you confine yourself to a maximum of twenty hooks.

Curl the line with hooks (size 4) baited round inside an old plastic washing-up bowl and try laying it first at low tide on the shore. Use a colossal weight on each end of the line and lay the line up the beach, not across it. If you lay it across the beach the incoming tide will try to drag it into a great loop.

Use a shore mark to make sure that you know exactly where you have put the line down. Some long-liners drive stakes into the beach to hold the line in position and these act as markers as well.

You must get up bright and early if you hope to collect your fish after the tide goes out. If you don't, not only do you run the risk of some even earlier riser finding your fish, but seagulls are big birds with very powerful beaks and one of them can make an awful mess of a fish.

The Beach Seine or Drag Net

There is yet another method of catching fish from the shore, but this one needs a large expenditure on equipment and so, unless you intend to take up this kind of fishing regularly or on every holiday, you may feel it is not justified.

I am referring to netting fish off the shore by means of a seine or drag net.

You will have to buy such a net unless you are skilled at net-making or are prepared to take time to learn. Basically, all you have to do, once you have the net, is to enlist the aid of a friend. Either he or you must wade out with one end of the net – it will not be necessary to go more than armpit deep – walk out in a circle and then return to the beach. Now the net is enclosing a half circle of water. The bottom end of the net is fitted with lead weights so that it sinks. The top of the net has plastic floats along its length. Now both of you start hauling in. Any fish in that area enclosed by your net are gradually driven in to the shore and finally pulled on to the beach in the net.

The length of the net varies of course, but

commercially made ones for the beach fisherman are usually thirty yards long by six feet deep or fifty yards long by nine feet deep. The art is in moving quietly when laying the net and keeping a steady haul going when recovering it. This method is very effective – particularly for mullet and sand eels.

I have seen sixty good-size grey mullet caught in one haul on the Sussex coast in October on an incoming tide. You could see other mullet escaping as the net came close in by jumping over the top. An old trick for stopping this is to sprinkle sawdust on the surface of the water inside the net. Apparently a mullet won't jump through a surface which it can't see through.

In Devon I have seen a similar operation net enough sand eels in one haul to satisfy all the waiting fishermen who wanted bait for their bass fishing. And there were enough left over to provide plenty of meals for anyone who fancied them. Sand eels are best fried as soon as possible after catching. Some people confuse them with whitebait, which are herring and sprat small fry. Sand eels have a different flavour. Remove the head and insides of the big ones, roll in flour, salt and then fry in butter or olive oil. Serve with lemon and lashings of white wine.

The cost of a seine net is about £48 for the thirty-yard version and £90 for a fifty-yard one. R. and B. Leakey of Belle Hill, Settle, Yorkshire can supply them.

11 Seaweed Snacks

The first time I ever ate seaweed it was on the same dish as the first limpet I ever ate raw. Both appeared on an 'assiette de mer' in a little restaurant not far from Le Touquet Airport. I must confess that I had been recommended to both the restaurant and the 'assiette', so I was not surprised at the contents of the dish. However, I was surprised, despite the recommendation, at how good both limpet and seaweed were.

Let me hasten to add that I am not suggesting that we should copy everything that the French eat – the way they roast beef should be declared a crime against the human palate! – but there's no harm in borrowing a little know-how now and then. In the case of the seaweed though, we Britons have been eating it quite as long as our Continental cousins, but you have to go out into the wilder parts of Britain to find it actually offered to you. In fact, the seaweed that was on my plate in Le Touquet all those years ago was what we call 'sea lettuce'. But we'll come to that in a moment.

The seaweeds that you'll find along the shore and can collect for food are simple to identify. You can use a book like Burke's *Marine Life*, (by W.D. Haas and F. Knorr) but many other books about the seashore will help you. All seaweeds are basically edible but some more than others. The following are worth trying.

Sea Lettuce (Fig. 23)
This one is known by other names, such as green laver, but its Latin name is the one to go by when

looking it up in reference books – *Ulva lactuca*. There is some resemblance to lettuce, but it does not have the crispness that we have come to expect from land lettuces. You'll find it in rock pools. Light green and delicate, it grows up to 2 feet long. If you find it when wading in deeper water, the colour will be much darker.

In Norway and Sweden it is eaten as salad, raw with lemon juice. In Brittany and other parts of the northern French coast it is served raw with other seafood.

Sometimes in parts of Britain it is served hot after being boiled. Vinegar is said to improve the flavour. Fried in bacon fat it can be served as a savoury on toast.

I am indebted to Carola Dickinson's book *British Seaweeds* (Eyre and Spottiswoode) for this gem about sea lettuce: 'Sir J.E. Smith (1759-1828) commenting on its popularity at fashionable tables says: "We suspect it to have been originally contrived with a medical intention, for the benefit of scrophulous patients, how numerous alas! in the gay circles of the opulent and great."'

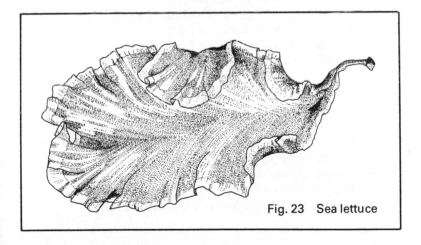

Fig. 23   Sea lettuce

Purple Laver

Sometimes called red laver (*Porphyra umbilicalis*). This is the famous one that produces 'laver bread'. You'll find it on the rocks near low water. It grows to 8 inches long and is usually purple or purple-red. However, it can take on greenish tinges on its ribbon-like lobes, which are very thin and often slit. It is at its best during the autumn months and can grow quite high up on the shore.

In Japan, where they are very much into seaweeds, the Porphyra family are cultivated specially for food, and these seaweeds are dried into thin sheets in which other foods like rice are wrapped – the equivalent of the British bread roll.

In Britain, you'll find laver bread most popular in South Wales, Ireland and North Devon. It's probably an acquired taste, but the 'bread' is said to be rich in vitamins B and C. In Ireland and the North-West, laver bread is sometimes called 'sloke'.

To prepare purple laver, wash carefully until all sand has been removed. Boil first then simmer for two to three hours until weed is tender. Drain, add butter and serve as a vegetable.

To make 'laver bread': Boil until a pulp. Now you will have a brownish-black jelly. Coat with oatmeal and fry in hot bacon fat on both sides. It is usually eaten with mashed potatoes.

Dulse

This is sometimes called sheepweed. The name comes from the sheep kept in the north-west of Scotland, which will browse along the shore at low tide. The sheep probably like the salty flavour of this weed (*Rhodymenia palmata*), which is called 'dillisk' in Ireland. It is a very common purple-red weed growing to a length of about 10 inches.

In years gone by it used to be used by sailors like chewing-tobacco or chewing gum.

The fan-like fronds can be eaten raw in this way but it is usually employed as a vegetable after being fried, or boiled in milk, or sautéed in butter after boiling until tender.

Irish Moss

Better known in some areas as carragheen, this flat weed (*Chondrus crispus*) is usually branched and forked and varies in colour from bright-red to dark-purple. It grows up to 8 inches long and can be eaten raw, though it is usually boiled. You will find it on rocks or small stones.

If you boil it for any length of time you will find that a thick jelly is formed. This can be used to make jellies (add your own fruit and sugar), blancmanges, sauces and soups, and sometimes serves as a substitute for aspic when making meat moulds.

And finally, I can't resist adding the seaweed called. . .

Dabberlocks

You shouldn't miss this one – the fronds can grow 6 feet long but as you only want to eat the middle ribs of young plants, you must not be greedy! The dabberlocks is also known as the bladderlocks, murlin, henware and even winged kelp, but they are all *Alaria esculenta*. Long olive-yellow fronds with tiny brown spots. It is said they taste of radish.

One last thought: in this book I have tried to show how much food is available on our British beaches. I have not covered every single item it is possible to eat. For example, the common beadlet anemone – that red blob which is seen on so many rocks on the shore – and the snakelocks anemone, whose tentacles decorate many rock pools, are quite edible. The French make fritters out of them – calling the larger one 'tomatoes of the sea' – but their preparation needs great care because of the stinging cells. For that reason I have avoided suggesting that you should eat them, and I only mention them now to show you that the amount of food awaiting your attention on the beach is almost limitless.

Index

Aberdeen, 57
anemones, 123, 124
assiettes de mer, 65

bacon, 47, 48
barnacles, 13
bass, 117
Bowden, Geoff, 104
Bridport-Gundry, 42
Brixham, 60
Burnham-on-Crouch, 26, 27, 57
byssus, 90

carpet shells, 99
catch-bag, 14
Channel, English, 57
clam chowder, 105
clams, 98 *et seq.*
cockles, 94 *et seq.*
compass, 12
conger eel, 37, 115
crabs:
   angry, 64
   baits, 60
   cooking, 61
   edible, 56 *et seq.*
   fiddler, 64
   freezing, 61
   hooks, 59
   killing of, 61
   lady, 65
   legal size, 57, 58
   pea, 92
   sauce, 63
   shore, 62
   soup, 63
   spider, 65 *et seq.*
   velvet, 64

Cromer, 57

dabberlocks, 123
Dartmouth, 57
Dickinson, Carola, 121
drag-net, 118
drop-netting, 50 *et seq.*
dulse, 122

fog, 12
footwear, 13
Fowey, 33
French chalk, 17

gapers, 100
gloves, 31
Gugen, Oscar, 18
Gweek Estuary, 91

Irish moss, 123

Kingswear, 57

laver bread, 122
Leakey, R.D., 47, 75
Leigh-on-Sea, 95
limpets, 107 *et seq.*
Lincoln, 95
lobsters:
   bait, 45
   berried, 28, 29
   common, 25 *et seq.*
   cooking, 53
   freezing, 54, 55
   hooks, 35 *et seq.*
   killing of, 52
   legal size, 28
   pots, 39 *et seq.*

long-lining, 117
Lytham, 84

McDonald, Joanna, 87
McDonald, Penny, 18
mask, 21 *et seq.*
Morecambe, 84, 95
mullet, 119
mussels:
  common, 88 *et seq.*
  cooking, 93
  horse, 92

neoprene, 15
Norfolk, 28, 57
Northumberland, 28, 56

O'Farrell, R.C., 47
otter shells, 99

plaice, 117
Plymouth, 57
pool-fishing, 115, *et seq.*
prawns:
  common, 70 *et seq.*
  cooking, 80
  freezing, 81
  nets, 74 *et seq.*
  pots, 78 *et seq.*
  sizes, 73

razor clams, 102 *et seq.*

Salcombe, 32, 91
sand-eels, 119

sand-gaper, 100
seine-net, 118
shellfish:
  laboratory, 26, 57
  safety, 88, 89
  soup, 68
Sheringham, 57
shrimps:
  common, 82 *et seq.*
  cooking, 86
  freezing, 86
  nets, 85
  pots, 86
  potted, 86
  sizes, 84
Sidmouth, 33
spat, 91
sterilization, 88, 89
sunglasses, 21

tapes, 99
tides, 11, 12

Venus shells, 101
viewing-box, 23

Walcheren, 90
Wales, 57
weever fish, 86, 87
Western Highlands, 72
whelks, 111 *et seq.*
Whitby, 57
winkles, 109 *et seq.*
Wood, Gerald, 33

Yonge, C.M., 90